Life Lessons from a Bad Quaker

LIFE LESSONS

FROM A

BAD QUAKER

A Humble Stumble Toward
Simplicity and Grace

J. BRENT BILL

ABINGDON PRESS

NASHVILLE

LIFE LESSONS FROM A BAD QUAKER
A HUMBLE STUMBLE TOWARD SIMPLICITY AND GRACE

Copyright © 2016 by J. Brent Bill

Macro Editor: Holly Halverson

Published in association with Books & Such Literary Agency

Library of Congress Cataloging-in-Publication Data

Bill, J. Brent, 1951-
Life lessons from a bad Quaker : a humble stumble toward simplicity and grace / J. Brent Bill.—First [edition].
        pages cm
Includes bibliographical references.
ISBN 978-1-63088-131-3 (binding: soft back)   1. Society of Friends.   2. Conduct of life.
I. Title.
BX7731.3.B55 2016
248.4'896—dc23

2015026963

16 17 18 19 20 21 22 23 24—10 9 8 7 6 5 4 3 2 1
MANUFACTURED IN THE UNITED STATES OF AMERICA

To Lil Copan
An honorary Bad Friend
and great friend

Contents

INTRODUCTION

"Nothing Is Better for Thee Than We." That was the tagline to an ad I wrote when I was a young hotshot denominational executive out to singlehandedly revive Quakerism. It was a play on Quaker Oats motto at the time—"Nothing is better for thee than me." The ad also featured a row of Quaker Oats boxes sitting above the words "These aren't the only Quakers in town." I'd show it to you except that I can't. For reasons you'll soon discover.

It was pretty clever, if I do say so myself. Another one of my oh-so-quirky ads featured an old broad-brim hat and the words, "Quakers aren't old hat." A third one had pictures of a car and horse and buggy inviting the reader to "Check the latest in Quaker transportation." All firmly tongue-in-cheek, they gave a bit of information about us and invited people to visit their local groups.

Why was reviving Quakerism important to me? Because the Quaker way saved my life.

I grew up in the Religious Society of Friends, as Quakers are formally known. I didn't fully choose it as my spiritual path, though, until I was a college student. Even though I was an art major, I took lots of religion classes—including ones about Quakerism. Through those classes, the books assigned, and a kind, fierce, funny professor who became one of my mentors, I encountered a way of faith and life that spoke to my heart and soul. I found a faith path that worked for me.

This peculiar (and I do mean peculiar) faith provided me with tools I needed to live well. Well, at least better. As a guy whose brain was full of chattering monkeys constantly swinging from one tree limb of thought to the next, it taught me stillness. As a hothead (just ask any of the umpires or referees from hundreds of softball and basketball games I played or coached in), I slowly learned the way of peace. This faith tradition and its practices brought out my best, helped me work on my worst, and fed my soul.

Not that it made me perfect. As a young adult when I worked on those ads, I couldn't brook any criticism. I was too arrogant for my own good. My marriage was falling apart. I was a real stinker. Still, I'd have been an even bigger stinker if I hadn't been a Quaker. If it helped me that much, maybe it would help others, too.

Soon, those ads began attracting attention. Local newspapers and television stations called for interviews. They found something novel in the idea that Quakers advertised. That and they discovered we had a sense of humor, too. My odd little advertising story was picked up by the wire news services and went national.

I was pretty pleased with my humble self.

Then came a thick envelope from a Chicago law firm. As I read the letter inside, I soon saw that it came from an attorney representing the Quaker Oats Company. In legal but clear language, he told me to knock off any use of photographs of Quaker Oats boxes, facsimiles of Quaker Oats boxes, cartoons of Quaker Oats boxes, my kids' drawings of Quaker Oats boxes...you get the idea. Also to quit using variations of the "Nothing is better for thee than me." *Or else what?* I wondered. The "or else" became clear: they'd sue me down to my little Quaker grey socks.

After composing a number of witty rejoinders and tearing them up,

I pulled the Quaker Oats–related ads. I was arrogant, but not stupid. "Quaker Oats Sues Quaker" sounded like a great David and Goliath story—but this David had neither slingshot nor very deep pockets.

That was thirty years ago. A lot has changed. I'm no longer young. I'm a bit less arrogant. Instead of being a hotshot denominational executive, I'm better known in Friends circles as the cofounder of the Association of Bad Friends on Facebook. It's a humorous site for folks who are just not very good at being Quaker—folks who aren't always peaceable, humble, kind, loving, truthful, and all the other spiritual qualities for which Friends are known. If, that is, anybody even knows us at all.

I'm not just a bad Quaker, either. I'm a bad Christian, too. As my friend Diana Butler Bass reported in *A People's History of Christianity: The Other Side of the Story*: "'When someone asks me what kind of Christian I am,' says Brent Bill, a Quaker writer, 'I say I'm a bad one.' He goes on to say, 'I've got the belief part down pretty well, *When I say "bad," I mean I'm just bad at being good.* I think. It's in the practice of my belief in everyday life where I often miss the mark.'"

Now I'm not proud that I'm a bad Quaker. But I don't deny it. True, it's probably not the smartest thing for a guy who writes books about spirituality to admit. So you need to understand that by "bad," I don't mean *evil*. I don't have a bunch of bodies stashed in my trunk. I haven't robbed any banks. I have shot people (more about that later). When I say "bad," I mean I'm just bad at being good. Bad despite more than sixty years of attending Sunday school, worship services, summer camps, revivals, prayer meetings, retreats, workshops, religious colleges, seminary; being a pastor; reading spiritual books, writing spiritual books, and memorizing Bible verses. I stumble a lot!

But I'm better than I was. As I said earlier, that's thanks to things

I've learned following the Quaker way of living out being a friend of Jesus ("I call you friends"). It has helped me grow more into the person God and I want me to be. I'm a pilgrim, stumbling along the path toward grace and into the eternal presence of God.

For me, the lessons I've learned whilst on this humble stumble have helped me weave, with Divine assistance, a sort of protective covering for my life. Yeah, that sounds pretty strange—and nowhere close to Paul's "full armor of God." But hey, I'm already pretty warlike at times. So while Paul's armor analogy is a good, strong one, I need one that's gentler. One that teaches me the grace of God. Besides, armor has to be custom fitted and ready to put on before it's any good and I'm not much of a metal smith (just ask my seventh-grade shop teacher). But if I'm weaving a tapestry of listening to God, practicing peace and stillness, loving all, taking care of the earth, and extending equality, I find myself acquiring (in a good kind of acquisition) the fruits of the Spirit: "love, joy, peace, patience, kindness, goodness, faithfulness, gentleness, and self-control. There is no law against things like this." These form a tapestry that I can drape over me, even if it's not completely finished.

While spiritual stillness, peace, equality, community, et al., are not uniquely Quaker, the Friends have a unique take on them. I have learned that growing deep in the life of the Spirit doesn't take me out of the life I'm living. Instead, its spiritual tools and practices show me how to live better in this world—better for the world and for me. Through this unique take, I've learned a thing or three. Take peace, for example. It once was, for me, a theological idea and a spiritual ideal. Now the Quaker spin on peace as a matter of faith and daily living has transformed me from a mere believer in peace to a practitioner of peace. Except when someone cuts me off on the freeway. I'm still working on that.

I'm not the only one. Dame Judi Dench (star of screen and stage) was recently interviewed on British television. The interviewer asked, "Are you still a Quaker? Has it informed you? Are you a 'peacenik'?" She replied, "Yes. I think it informs everything I do.... I wouldn't be without it."

I wouldn't be without it either. Like Judi and me (all of us Friends are on a first-name basis, you know. That's why we're called Friends. Ha!), you may find the Quaker take on these familiar faith concepts and how to live them helpful, too.

I'm not trying to turn you into a Quaker. Not even a bad one, like me. You're welcome to remain the bad Episcopalian, bad Presbyterian, bad United Methodist, bad Anything, or bad Nothing you want to be. But just maybe what this bad Friend has learned will help a bit along your own humble stumble toward grace.

God knows I needed it.

I still do!

CHAPTER 1

JUST BE QUIET

Stillness for Those Too Busy to Sit Still

There is a quiet, open place in the depths of the mind, to which we can go many times in the day and lift up our soul in praise, thankfulness and conscious unity. With practise his God-ward turn of the mind becomes an almost constant direction, underlying all our other activities.
—Kenneth Boulding

Words may help and silence may help, but the one thing needful is that the heart should turn to its Maker as the needle turns to the pole. For this we must be still.
—Caroline Stephen

Listen carefully to what I am about to tell you.
—Jesus

"Shut up," he explained.
—Ring Lardner

I'm not good at being quiet. There. Got that out of the way. People assume that, since I'm a lifelong Quaker, I must have some genetic bent for staying silent—silence being a hallmark of Friends worship and witness, after all.

In fact, since I'm confessing to my badness, I may as well admit that when I first started writing this chapter, I opened a blank document—and iTunes. Stumble!

I live in the land of sound. I like it. When I built my house, I wired it for music and movie dialogue. When I bought my latest car, it came with AM, FM, satellite radio, a CD player, and a woman who reminds me when it's time to get my oil changed. No, not my wife, Nancy, but some other woman who lives in my dashboard and tells me what to do. And who is always right. Hmmm, maybe she is some relation to Nancy!

When I climb on my John Deere to mow between the rows of trees we planted to reforest the lower field and filter chemical runoff from farms around us, I put on ear protectors to keep out the droning diesel. Underneath the ear protectors, though, I usually slip a set of earbuds. I could go on, but you get the idea. In fact, you may live the idea. My life with sound might mirror yours.

I like my tunes, NPR talk radio, television shows. I also like bird song, urban noise, conversations, overheard conversations (bad!), and more. I fill my life with a fury of sound that signifies something: I just don't know how to be still.

Well, actually, I do. I just avoid it. Even though I know better. Now I'm not talking about the kind of quiet that my parents, grandparents, sisters, friends, bosses, neighbors, strangers on a plane, and others have been urging me to be. I'm talking about how to be deeply silent in my soul. Learning the art of spiritual stillness. Even after years of practicing it, I still forget to do it. That's mostly because I am so wrapped up in myself that I forget to be quiet. Especially quiet enough to hear God talking to me.

What about you?

When's the last time you were really quiet? Intentionally quiet? Spiritually quiet?

You're gonna find that I ask questions like that throughout our time together. That's because it's one of the main ways we odd Friends go deep and get to spiritual truth. Instead of giving answers, we ask questions. We invite each other to get quiet and hear God teaching us in our souls. So brace yourself—questions will keep coming.

The good news is there's no one right answer. Just give the answer that's honest to you and where you are. It may be comforting. It may be challenging. It may make you humble. Maybe even recall a stumble. It will move you further toward grace.

Stumbles in Bad Quaker History: Silence Would Have Been Golden

In October 1656, Quaker James Nayler and his friends went to Bristol, England, and reenacted the triumphal entry of Jesus into Jerusalem. Nayler rode on a donkey while his entourage sang "Holy, Holy, Holy" and strewed the muddy path with garments. The Puritans were not amused. They hauled him off his ass, tried him before parliament, found him guilty. They branded his forehead with the letter B for blasphemy and pierced his tongue with a hot iron to keep him silent. Oh, and then they tacked on two years of prison at hard labor.

HAVE YOU EVER HEARD GOD TALKING TO YOU?

Back in the seventies, I sang with a group that called itself "The Sure Foundation." TSF was a Youth for Christ musical group that was a sorta low-rent, very Christian version of the Spurrlows. (If you don't know the Spurrlows, just Google!) Yeah, while some of my friends and relatives were doing things that made them unable to remember the

3

seventies, I was doing music and other things I'd like to forget. I was bad at faith back then but (despite my long hair and normal mischievousness) was pretty straight. We—three sopranos, three altos, three tenors, three basses, a rhythm section, and a horn section—traveled around Ohio singing at youth rallies, for youth groups, in church services, and more. The things I'd like to forget are the cheesy songs (especially the musical "updates" of hymns such as "Love Lifted Me" and "Trust and Obey"), the really lousy matching polyester outfits we wore, and the few times they let me solo. My voice is not made for soloing!

One of my favorite songs from that time was "Did You Ever Hear God Speaking to You?" by Sonny Salisbury. It was upbeat, poppy, and asked if we'd ever heard God saying that we were needed if God's work was going to get done.

Now the phraseology isn't very…Godlike (it's hard to imagine Charlton Heston as God intoning "And I'll sure be needing you if it ever gets done" in a Cecil B. DeMille biblical blockbuster). But it is a good question.

If you happened by a Quaker meetinghouse on a Sunday morning (which would have to be by accident, since we always locate our meeting places on side streets, upstairs conference rooms, back alleys, or other hard-to-find locations) and looked in the windows, you'd most likely see a bunch of people sitting in a circle, heads bowed, and what looks like nothing much going on.

As YouTube's satirical church-hopper Betty Butterfield says of Quakers, "It was eighteen adults settin' in a circle. It was like an AA meeting, but nobody was sayin' nuthin.'"

Well, she's almost right. Maybe humans weren't sayin' nuthin', but God was. At least that's what we believe. That's why we shut up—to listen.

Many of us Quakers are naturally noisy people. While we're silent in worship, we talk a lot at other times. Just come to an after-worship potluck. Or a meeting for business! I admit that I'm a driven, Type-A personality. Yes, I'm one of the most annoying of the personality types. I'm much better at talking—especially giving directions—than listening. Especially listening for directions. Directions for me? I'd rather *talk* about God's directions for *you*!

Worshipful silence, though, is the way we still our inner and outer noise long enough to really listen for the God who says.... You might ask, "Says what?" That depends at least partly on us and what God knows we need to hear. God knows what I need to hear may not be what I want to hear! When we're silent and still, we sink down *I need silence. To remind me to listen! To God!* into a quiet that lets us feel the stirrings of the Spirit in our souls. Our inner ears open. Christ comes among us as we center in silence, just as He promised—"For where two or three are gathered in my name, I'm there with them." Christ comes to teach His people Himself. He most often teaches me in the deepest, richest, most silent part of my soul.

Now, I'm not saying that God speaks only when we're silent. Even a bad Quaker like me knows that God is speaking whether I'm listening or not. I'm a parent. I have often talked—very helpfully!—when my kids (and now their kids) weren't listening. All they heard was that rising and falling "wah-wah-wah" sound of an adult in a *Peanuts* cartoon. So even though God speaks to me constantly, I'm just not listening. That's why I need silence. To remind me to listen! To God!

God's getting our attention is not only a modern phenom. Just look at all the times God spoke to humans in the dead of night—to young Samuel, Mary, and more. Or sent angels to get people's attention. Or used a talking donkey.

But we can't always expect God to reach us via angelic visitation, heavenly dreams, or animals with the gift of speech. If I had to choose among the three, I'd take the heavenly dreams. Dreams I can handle. Mostly. Angels? From everything I've deduced, angel visitors must be somewhat scary. Sorta like Seth, the character Nicolas Cage played in *City of Angels*—black-clothed, brooding, and ominous. "Like a stalker," says my friend Stephanie. Indeed. Maybe that's why they always say "Be not afraid" when they show up.

I've always found talking animals a bit creepy, too. Even in cartoons. And Francis the Talking Mule of 1950s movie fame—who needs a talking donkey? Oh, I guess Balaam sorta did.

Well, I'm just glad God doesn't use clowns. I'd really freak then.

Now you might think that we Quakers came up with the whole idea of silence in a kinder, gentler, quieter time. Wrong! Friends started practicing spiritual silence in a time when religion was a blood sport. Literally—armies of religious soldiers fighting for their faith and against the other guys. A Friendly friend of mine says it was sort of like Jehovah's Witnesses with guns! Instead of *The Watchtower* it was "Watch out!" Men and women (at least the women were getting some equal rights!) were thrown into prison for their faith.

Between the gunfire and the theological arguing, the Quakers began worshiping in silence. They wanted to get beyond the clamor and opinion of theologians, Anglican priests, biblical scholars, Catholic priests, Puritan divines, and nonconformist preachers and hear directly from God. They weren't any holier or better than other Christians (well, admittedly, some of them thought they were). What they were was hungry for an immediate, direct experience of God. They found that they experienced that better as they settled into silence together and listened as one to the Divine.

That's why silence is important to Quakers today. It helps us listen. I, for one, need the reminder to listen that silence provides. Otherwise I'll be be-bopping through life wearing earbuds and oblivious that God is trying to get my attention.

QUICK QUAKER QUESTIONS

Remember, no one right answer. What's your soul say?

- Have I ever even considered the thought that getting quiet might be a good way to hear God?
- Have I ever listened carefully so that I could hear God?
- Have I ever heard God speaking? How did I know it was God?

OH, DO SHUT UP

That's a line from one of my favorite flicks—*A Fish Called Wanda*. There are a lot of "shut-ups" in that film. The people in it just didn't know how to do it. Let's face it, many of us don't. At least not anymore. We were probably at our quietest, in some ways, when we were kids. I was. Except for those times I was terrorizing the neighborhood or caught up in extracurricular classroom conversations, I often spent time quietly. Reading. Using my imagination. I see that in my grandchildren. It's we adults who are especially bad at being quiet. Even in circumstances that call for silence.

I was at a writing conference once where the emcee announced that Fred, who was a regular attendee and whom most people there knew, had died recently." We will now have a moment of silence in his memory." We no sooner bowed our heads than he excitedly announced the luncheon speaker. We didn't have a moment of silence. We had a nanosecond.

We need to learn to shut up. And shut out—the noise. The rush. The clamor and clatter.

But how?

One of the things I love doing is volunteering for a week to be a visiting pastor on Bald Head Island in North Carolina. While you might, as my grandchildren do, think it was named for me, it wasn't. I tend to talk about something sorta Quakerly during my week—on peace, simplicity, and so on. One thing I always do is include a period of waiting worship. I explain how our worship is rooted in silence. I also explain that we don't do *silent* worship—we're not worshiping the silence. Instead we do waiting worship—we wait on God to speak.

Now the folks who gather at the Village Chapel of Bald Head Island are not Quakers. They are a mix of Episcopal, United Methodist, Baptist (of various stripes), Catholic, and more. A Quaker occasionally shows up, but not often. So I'm always a bit nervous about asking the congregation to be quiet for five minutes to listen to God. Would it be like the writing conference? Or the fellow who came to dinner at a Friend's home and, when they sat down to eat, observed everyone just sitting there. "There was this really awkward silence," he said, "so I just told a little joke and broke the ice."

Sigh.

So, standing up front, looking out at the congregation, I got nervous. I wondered if I should skip or shorten the silence. So far the good people there had never failed to get quiet. I mean *quiet.*

We need intentional spaces.

No shuffling feet. No uncomfortable throat-clearing. Nothing but spiritual listening.

Following the benediction, as folks filed out of the church, more people than I could count said something like, "Thank you for the silence. I needed that."

Don't we all? We need intentional silent spaces.

So one way you can begin to learn the way of spiritual silence is to create your own space for it—and then invite yourself to attend.

Dear (insert your name here)—

God cordially invites you to attend a period of listening silence at 10 a.m. this morning. No RSVP needed.

That may seem sorta silly, but it is one way to get started. Then you follow it by actually creating space. For me, it means making two kinds—a physical space and a permission space.

Let's start with the second one. If you're like me, you may think that taking time to be quiet means not doing anything. It may be what someone peering in our windows would think (but then what are they doing looking in our windows?). Society teaches us that productive, useful people do not just sit there. Besides, there are a million things to do: mow the grass, do the laundry, do the work someone's paying us to do, wax the cat, write a book on sitting in silent listening.

So the first thing you're going to have to do is give yourself permission to stop! Stop, sit down, be quiet. I could give you all kinds of reasons why it is perfectly okay for *you* to sit in silence. I have to tell myself that it's more than okay to take some time with God. If I'm going to try to live Jesus' way, it might help for me to hear a little bit from Jesus. I remind myself that all that to-do stuff will be there when I get back. It's not going anywhere (no matter how much I wish some of it would). Well, that's not completely true. Sometimes it does go away when I get quiet and listen for and to God—because an answer that Spirit has been waiting to give me arrives in the silence. An answer that I didn't hear in the noise. So it's completely okay, as a person of humble, stumbling faith, to quiet my soul and listen for the voice of the One Who Loves Me More Than I Know.

You have permission, too. I give you permission. If anybody asks, just say, "Brent Bill, head of the Bad Quakers, said I could take a couple of minutes to listen to God." Who's gonna argue with that? Well, the last part anyhow. Kinda hard to rag on someone who's listening for God.

Except for your boss or kids or someone else who thinks he or she is God.

I'm not suggesting that you start by giving yourself permission to take a week off for silence. Not that you could keep in silence that long! But you could give yourself permission to take five minutes. Five minutes isn't much. It's enough, though, to settle your body and mind. To breathe deep. To be aware of tension in your body and soul. And to say, like young Samuel, "Speak. Your servant is listening." Or, if you don't care for the servant language, ask, "What do You want to say to me?"

Decide the best time for you. It doesn't need to be the most convenient time (though it's easier to justify it when it is). What's the *best* time? For me it's between 10:00 and 10:05 a.m. I don't have a very long "best" time. When could you get the most out of silent listening? When will it refresh you the most?

- Before the rest of the family gets up?
- After the family goes to sleep?
- After they've headed off to school or work or...?
- At work, during your scheduled break?

Notice I didn't ask, What's the most convenient time? If I picked the most convenient time, it would be between 9:55 and 9:56 p.m.— right before I drift off to sleep. But I don't need the silence so much then. Besides, God has all night to visit me in my dreams. I need the silence in the midst of my busyness. My overbusyness. At the times I think, *I just can't take time for silence right now.* Which is the same as saying, "I don't have time for You right now, God."

Major stumble. A fall-down-the-spiritual-stairs sorta stumble.

That's not something I (or you) would say to someone we love deeply. We'd make time. Happily. Be thrilled to see or hear that person. Because we love him or her and we're loved in return. Taking time for that person gives us a sense of spaciousness we didn't have before.

So...permission granted for silence. By love.

Second, pick a physical place for silence. For me, it's often in my office. Walking in the woods in the late afternoon is another good silent place for me. Or during the week I spend each month in Philadelphia working in the central Quaker offices, it's in the quiet car on the Chestnut Hill East line into Center City.

There is no "right" place. There's just a right-for-you place—relaxing in your easy chair in the corner of the living room by the window that has your favorite view, while enjoying a garden or city park, sitting in your car in a corner of a church parking lot on a busy street before going into work.

The possibilities of permission and place are limited solely by your imagination and desire. Unless, of course, you'd really rather be bad than good.

QUICK QUAKER QUESTIONS

Remember, no one right answer. What's your soul say?

- So what's the ideal time for me to listen for God?
- Where could I listen the best?
- What makes them a good time and place? What about that time and place will help me connect to the Divine?

Stumbles in Bad Quaker History: Silence Is Golden—And Unindictable

During the Watergate investigation involving Quaker president Richard M. Nixon, a series of nine secretly recorded tapes was subpoenaed. Before they could be turned over, an 18½ minute gap on the tapes was discovered. While what had been originally recorded in that gap was never known, most people do not think it was Richard M. Nixon giving vocal ministry, which is when a Quaker stands out of the silence and offers a message. He offered vocal something... but not ministry.

Do Not Get Thee to a Nunnery

Once when I was working on my sermon and order of worship for my week on Bald Head Island, I thought I'd speak on silence.

Sounds pretty silly, doesn't it? Well, silliness has never stopped me from doing anything. I picked some scriptures and wrote a wonderfully deep and powerful sermon about silence.

When I got to the island, I learned that the group The Elements of Praise, from Pitt Community College, would provide special music for the service. The Elements of Praise, I learned, was a gospel choir. *This may mean some tweaking on my part*, I thought. I'm not sure spirited gospel music was going to fit with my plan for a contemplative experience of spiritual silence. (Yay, a rare humble moment.) Then on Sunday morning, when I arrived at the chapel and heard them warming up, I thought, *This is going to mean some real spiritual tweaking.*

This listening through life—even in a worship service that's carefully planned and prepared—is what Friendly silence is about.

As the choir processed in, in the midst of their powerful rendition of "What If God Is Unhappy with Our Praise?" the choir members' voices filled the space and left no room for other audible sound. Instead I heard them in my heart: *Put aside what you were going to say and follow the Spirit's movement.*

Now for this pastor to hear the word to lay aside his carefully structured order of worship, scripture readings, and—gasp—sermon, well, let me tell you, that's just plain hard. Especially since I too often put a high value on intellect and order and not enough on listening to the Spirit and flowing in the moment.

But that morning I got it right. Sort of. I told the congregation that we Quakers did silence so we could hear the word of God in the moments of everyday life. And obey it. And that the word of God to me was to follow the spiritual leading of the spiritual singers. And to throw away the bulletin because it really didn't matter at that point.

I found a new call to worship. I came up with a new scripture. I spoke on the kin-dom of God and the joyous way God speaks to us in fresh ways. We had a worship time of soulful silences and soul-filled singing. Clapping. An amen or five. The Spirit was alive and moving through that congregation—because we all listened together through the silences of soul as we sang aloud. Yep, I'm proud to say it was one of my humbles, not stumbles.

This listening through life—even in a worship service that's carefully planned and prepared—is what Friendly silence is about. This kind of silence doesn't always require me to get away to a quiet place, like alone by the seashore or a silent retreat at a monastery. Rather it's carrying spiritual stillness in my soul as I move through life. The beauty of Quaker silence is that it can be practiced wherever we are. It doesn't matter whether we're rockin' to some gospel numbers in a quaint island chapel more used to Bach fugues than Harry T. Burleigh spirituals or working on the assembly line in a computer factory. Deep spiritual stillness, listening down to our souls is not dependent on silent surroundings. It's about stillness inside us.

I find that really good news. For lots of reasons. Not least of which is that I have always needed to make a living and support my family. So I need a faith, the practices of which are rooted in the common stuff of daily life and don't require me to zip off to someplace special to practice them.

It's not that I dislike spiritual retreats. They are a wonderful means of going deep with God. And I especially enjoy those that offer long stretches of silence. But what I need is a faith that sustains me in the midst of daily life. One that I can practice while I'm living; I mean right in the middle of the business of my life. In fact, it's really helpful to have it right when life is even more hectic than I can imagine. I need to know that I can use Quaker silence to center myself. Right then. I don't have to wait until Sunday morning or the upcoming silent retreat.

It's a way, says Thomas Kelly, one of the great guides of the interior life,

> of conducting our inward life so that we are perpetually bowed in worship, while we are also very busy in the world of daily affairs.... This practice is the heart of religion. It is the secret, I am persuaded, of the inner life of the Master of Galilee. He expected this secret to be freshly discovered in everyone who would be his follower.

Busy outwardly, centered and silently inwardly. Speaking from experience, it's not gonna happen overnight. Amazon Prime is not going to ship it via drone for same-day delivery. It comes from practice.

So if you want some good advice from a bad Quaker (do as I say, not always as I do), start with the next time you're really swamped. You're in deep and the alligators are up to your neck...and drawing closer. You can, as I often do, go into full panic mode. Or you can take a breath. A breath doesn't keep the gators from circling nearer. But the physical act of a breath as a spiritual exercise reminds us that we are not in control of the situation.

That may not be what you wanted to hear. I certainly don't like hearing that! But the fact is, even though at my deepest level I know I'm not in control, I often live as if I think I am. And so I bull my way through and soon run out of resources.

My wife, Nancy, often tells me to breathe. She sees me super involved in writing a book, doing farm work, whatever. I'm figuring it all out and am physically busy, busy, busy. When she tells me to breathe, what she's really telling me is to settle and trust.

When I listen to that advice, I begin in a millisecond of silence to invite God back into my life. Not that God has left, but I've certainly shut the door and limited the healing, guiding contact that communication with the Divine provides. When I breathe I reengage with the God who is always with me.

A good thing about this silence is that it is not disturbed by the monkeys chattering around in our brains. In fact, it invites them into itself. There it washes them, spins them around while shaking off the excess, and lays them out where they can be seen clearly. It often gives me a spiritual suggestion or three on how to now deal with them.

So, when you're first practicing silence in the midst of daily life, don't worry that disparate thoughts and concerns keep popping up. Don't regard them as intrusions. Embrace them as part of your life with God.

My friend Doug Pagitt told me that at his church, Solomon's Porch in Minneapolis, instead of telling people to turn off or silence their cell phones during worship, he invites those who gather to leave on their cell phones. Real life should intrude in worship. Worship should intrude in real life. Faith isn't much good if it can't stand alongside all our busyness and offer good words and guidance.

So take a breath.

Get silent in your soul.

Invite God to reengage with you there.

Listen for that which runs deep and sticks. That which satisfies. All the time while doing the laundry, catching up on e-mails, working on a presentation, driving in rush hour, whatever. Silence in the shape of your heart can become an active, constant communion with the great Lover of your soul.

QUICK QUAKER QUESTIONS

Remember, no one right answer. What's your soul say?

- What clues does my body give me that I need a deep spiritual breath and some stillness in the midst of busyness?

- How might a good word from God help me?
- How might a hard word from God help me? (Yikes!)

A SILENCE SABBATH

"True silence is the rest of the mind; and is to the spirit, what sleep is to the body, nourishment and refreshment." That's what William Penn said centuries ago. Many Americans think that the guy on the Quaker Oats box is William Penn, for whom Pennsylvania was named. Except it's not and it wasn't. Pennsylvania was named for William's father (Admiral William Penn) and nobody knows who the man on the oats box is (though I've heard he's referred to as Larry at the Quaker Oats offices).

William Penn was one of the first Friends. There are times I think that he wrote this statement about silence after seeing Friends snoring softly in Meeting. If so, he's not the only one. Benjamin Franklin (who many people think was a Quaker because he dressed funny) wrote about this happening on his first visit to Philadelphia.

> [I] walked again up the street, which by this time had many clean-dressed people in it, who were all walking the same way. I joined them, and thereby was led into the great meeting-house of the Quakers near the market. I sat down among them, and, after looking round awhile and hearing nothing said, being very drowsy thro' labor and want of rest the preceding night, I fell fast asleep, and continued so till the meeting broke up, when one was kind enough to rouse me. This was, therefore, the first house I was in, or slept in, in Philadelphia.

Despite Franklin's sleeping in meeting, Penn probably had Jesus' statement in mind—"Come to me, all you who are struggling hard and carrying heavy loads, and I will give you rest." Who among us—mother, father, coworker, boss—is not struggling and burdened? Whose soul doesn't need nourishment and refreshment? Words and phrases like *burnout, chronic fatigue syndrome*, and *stressed-out* fill our conversations. Silence invites us to rest in God's loving care, a loving care so restful that some fall asleep.

Need some rest? I do!

I find that a Sabbath for silence is a good place to get that rest that I need. I need my rest! You really don't want to be around me if I didn't get my eight or nine hours of sleep the night before. So I take a Sabbath of silence. I shut up. Turn the tap off for a while. I re-center amid the hectic pace that is my life. I quiet down to hear the voice of God and reorient my soul a bit. I check what words I'm really going to need to say and which I need to lay aside.

For me that often starts by disconnecting electronically. Gasp! Not shutting off the computer, iPad, iPhone!? 'Fraid so. As I work on this book I'm surrounded by gadgets that are sending me streams of communication and live connections to Facebook, Twitter, FourSquare, LinkedIn, and more.

I start my Sabbaths of silence by posting a notice on Facebook ("I'm going to be quiet now. My soul needs it. Ta-ta"). I set the auto reply on my e-mail programs (all three of them!) to say that I'm taking a silence break and will be back in touch soon. And then I begin shutting things down. I turn my chair toward the window if I'm at home. I go for a walk if I'm in Center City, Philadelphia.

Yes, I'm still swathed in sound. Internal and external. But slowly, as I strip away the sounds that *I've* added to my life, calming comes. Extraneous sounds, within and without, fade. My breathing deepens. I come more fully into a place of attention to the Divine.

It's in such a holy silence that I come to know the Living Word, as the Gospel writer John calls Jesus. In the silence I come to the Living Word of God directly—the Word that the writer of Hebrews tells us "is living, active, and sharper than any two-edged sword. It penetrates to the point that it separates the soul from the spirit and the joints from the marrow. It's able to judge the heart's thoughts and intentions."

And my soul often needs that piercing—a cutting directly to the heart of the matter. Or matters. Taking a silence Sabbath takes me to a place in my soul where I stand naked in spirit before God. Now I don't much like being naked anywhere! Especially soulfully naked in front of God. But being stripped bare of all spiritual pretense humbles me. I can stumble on my own. I find it hard to be humble without God's assistance.

Naked in silence before the Divine is when God gives me more power for living my faith. In the silence I perceive God's work in me being slowly realized. Anytime I come into God's presence, I leave ready to live out the gospel. Not just with a good intention, but with, as the old revivalists used to say, "Holy Ghost power." If, that is, I take time—and not just a quick hit of silence—to be still.

"The contemplative," says Thomas Merton, "is not merely a man who likes to sit and think." The purpose of contemplation, he continues, is "to entertain silence in my heart and listen for the voice of God."

Listening to God's voice has no point and no reality unless it's firmly rooted in daily life. Listening silences created by prayer overflow with God's presence. They fill us with a wonder and power that helps us live in our world. Listening silences lead us into living more simply, treating others more justly, caring for the earth more deeply, and more. That's because in the listening silences we hear the Voice.

Now that Voice might speak encouragement. A word of hope.

Or a word of condemnation.

I thought about that while reading my Bible the other day. I came across these verses:

> Woe to you, you teacher and writer of spirituality books, you Quaker, you hypocrite! You are like a whitewashed tomb, you look beautiful on the outside but on the inside you are full of the bones of the dead and everything

unclean. In the same way, on the outside you appear to people as righteous but on the inside you are full of hypocrisy and wickedness...and sometimes bad writing. (Matthew 23:27–28 NBBV—New Brent Bill Version)

Ouch! Really, Jesus, was that necessary? Evidently. Because that eternal Voice tells us the things we need to hear, whether we like them or not. Christ calls us to transformation and faithfulness in every part of our lives. The words of God call us to love what God loves—all of creation and everything and everyone a part of it. That's because God made it all and pronounced it good. God's voice heard in stillness invites us into that goodness. It also invites us to work with God in bringing restoration and love to God's beloved creation.

Merton reminds us, "Contemplation is...the response to a call: a call from Him Who has no voice, and yet Who speaks in everything that is, and Who, most of all, speaks in the depths of our being: for we ourselves are words of His."

It is a voice that, when silent and still, even a bad guy like me can hear. And recognize. Even if it makes me squirm every now and then.

CHAPTER 2

WORLD AT WAR

Forget the Middle East—How Do I Get Along with My
Family, Coworkers, and Annoying Neighbors?

*We utterly deny all outward wars and strife and fightings with outward
weapons, for any end or under any pretence whatsoever. And this is our
testimony to the whole world... and we do certainly know, and so testify
to the world, that the spirit of Christ, which leads us into all Truth, will
never move us to fight and war against any man with outward weapons.*
—A Quaker Declaration to Charles II

*Our life is love, and peace, and tenderness; and bearing one with
another, and forgiving one another, and not laying accusations one
against another; but praying one for another, and helping one another
up with a tender hand.*
—Isaac Penington

*Happy are people who make peace,
Because they will be called God's children.*
—Jesus

You can't say that civilization don't advance…
in every war they kill you in a new way.
—Will Rogers

My career as a killer commenced as a kid. By the time I was thirteen I had slain each member of my immediate family (I had offed one of my sisters numerous times), countless cousins, a number of my adult neighbors, and a slew of strangers.

I amassed a pretty high body count—especially for a Quaker.

My weapon of choice was a gun. I picked my victims off with my Mattel Fanner 50, rubber-band guns, ping-pong-ball squeeze guns, water pistols, wooden flintlocks, Thompson submachine guns, James Bond Walther PPKs with silencers, my finger, and more. The Indian head ornament perched on the hood of my grandfather's Pontiac Star Chief made a perfect sight for the twin .50 caliber machine guns that he was unaware were mounted in the bumpers. The last murder I remember committing was in Tijuana. I shot a person taking my picture right after I'd purchased the gun I'm pointing at her. "No witnesses" was my motto. Though I still have the picture…and my sister with the camera is still alive. I was a pint-sized personage of death and destruction taking potshots at anybody I wished. From a faith perspective, it didn't bother me much. Killing people and being a good Christian didn't seem to be in opposition. Many of the heroes of the Bible we read about in First Day school (which is the Quaker way of saying Sunday school) were men of war or killing—Moses, Samson, Saul, Joshua, David, and more. Even some women got in on the act—Deborah, as one of the judges of Israel, set up a battle with Sisera, a general who had been oppressing the Israelites. Defeated in battle, Sisera took refuge in Heber's (an ally) tent. Jael, Heber's wife, invited him in, gave him something to drink, covered him with a blanket, and then drove a tent peg through his head while he slept, killing him.

Ouch!

And while I'd heard that Quakers were supposedly a peaceful people, that wasn't so much my experience of them. At least the group of Friends I grew up in. Whole hordes of church and family members served in the Army, Navy, and Army Air Corps. Especially during the "good war"—World War II. Many of my friends' fathers had been in the military, too.

While my killing rampage tapered off drastically in my teens (I found pursuing girls much more interesting), I didn't think about war that much. Even though it was raging around me—the Warsaw Pact invaded Czechoslovakia, the Israelis raided the Beirut airport, Nigeria was in revolt, and of course there was the Vietnam War. Mr. Oblivious, I was.

Finally, as I neared high school graduation and my own "opportunity" to serve, I began to think. The Vietnam War was at its bloodiest—at least for the United States. Getting drafted into the army didn't sound like a good career trajectory for me. I mean, during my senior year of high school, almost seventeen thou- *I was afraid to fight. I was afraid I might like fighting too much.* sand Americans died in the war. While I was morally ambiguous about shooting—really shooting—another human being, I knew I didn't want to be shot myself! I was self-centered that way.

Then came May 4. Just one week before my birthday. Just up the road from where I attended college. On that day members of the Ohio National Guard fired sixty-seven rounds in thirteen seconds into unarmed protesters (the closest of whom was one hundred feet away), some of whom were throwing rocks and National Guard tear gas canisters back at guardsman. Four students died. Nine others were wounded. Two of those killed weren't even protesters—just students walking to class. One of them was a member of the Army ROTC!

"Collateral damage," as the Pentagon says today.

I was afraid to fight.

I was afraid I might like fighting too much.

I had a hard time wrapping my head around the idea that, if drafted, I might be called on to shoot my fellow citizens. I mean, shooting foreigners in a jungle was one thing! But our own people? I also knew I might just do it if they riled me up enough. Throw some rock at me and I might just do more than point my M1 Garand rifle at you. Rock may beat scissors. But a .30-06 bullet beats rock. And kills you.

That second fear scared me. What if I did like it—a lot? And went on a real killing spree—even if it was sanctioned by my nation? I'd read Luke 22:49–51:

> When Jesus' follower saw what was going to happen, Brent said, "Lord, whom do You want me to shoot?" And then Brent fired and struck the servant of the high priest, shooting off his right ear.
>
> But Jesus answered, "No more of this, you doofus!" And He touched the man's ear and healed him. (NBBV)

Reading the Bible always gets me in trouble.

While I'd always taken my Christian faith seriously (very seriously, for someone who was so bad at it), I began trying to figure out if faith meant something in my day-to-day life. Not in the abstract. Not for others. For me. Especially around the issues of peace and war. A question that kept coming was, *Whom would Jesus shoot?*

I'd often told a joke about a Quaker farmer who, awakened one night by the sound of a burglar coming up the stairs, grabbed his shotgun, pointed it down the stairway, and proclaimed, "Friend Burglar, I would not harm thee for the world, but thee is standing where I'm about to shoot!" I wasn't so certain that my faith would let me shoot where anybody might be standing. Burglar or anybody else. This despite my willingness as a kid to liquidate anybody who merely annoyed me.

My move toward peace and away from mass murder and solo soldiering was furthered when I came across the words of seventeenth-century Quaker Robert Barclay:

> Whoever can reconcile this, "Resist not evil", with "Resist violence by force", again, "Give also thy other cheek", with "Strike again"; also "Love thine enemies", with "Spoil them, make a prey of them, pursue them with fire and the sword", or, "Pray for those that persecute you, and those that calumniate you", with "Persecute them by fines, imprisonments and death itself", whoever, I say, can find a means to reconcile these things may be supposed also to have found a way to reconcile God with the Devil, Christ with Antichrist, Light with Darkness, and good with evil. But if this be impossible, as indeed it is impossible, so will also the other be impossible, and men do but deceive both themselves and others, while they boldly adventure to establish such absurd and impossible things.

Yeah, the language is stilted, but I caught the drift. I couldn't make those things fit together. For me they were at completely opposite ends of the war/peace spectrum. So what was an eighteen-year-old boy to do? Forget the hypothetical eighteen-year-old—what would I do if drafted?

Would I fight and deny my slowly growing faith and belief that as a follower of Jesus I shouldn't shoot anybody?

Would I serve as noncombatant?

The issue was decided on the draft lottery of July 1, 1970. My birth-date was number 293. I was beyond the range of those who would be called.

Josiah Strong once said there is a popular faith that "God takes care of children, fools and the United States." I don't believe God takes special care of the United States, but God seemed to take care of this poor fool at that time. Perhaps to give me time to work on my decidedly unpeaceful nature.

QUICK QUAKER QUESTIONS

Remember, no one right answer. What's your soul say?

- What does it mean for me to be a peaceful person?
- How do I find ways to live peacefully in my daily relationships?
- Is my participation in war ever justified?

Stumbles in Bad Quaker History: Fight, Fight, Inner Light!

Nathanael Greene (1742–1786) was one of the Revolutionary War's "fighting Quakers." He was a major general in the Continental Army and George Washington's second-in-command. A year after attending a 1773 military parade, he organized a militia in Rhode Island and was promptly "disowned" (expelled) from his Quaker meeting.

"GO! FIGHT! QUAKERS!"

Every time I hear these three words my blood runs cold. Well, actually, it doesn't. I've already noted my war-mongering inner nature. Usually I laugh when I hear it. And in our school district, I have opportunities to hear it a lot—at football games, basketball games, wrestling matches, track and field events, the local grocery, and more. That's because our town was founded by Quakers back in the early nineteenth century. All our high school's athletic teams are named the Quakers. Our mascot is a burly little Quaker-type, though he's dressed in red, white, and blue—all colors shunned in early years by the black- and grey-dressing Friends.

He also looks as if he's ready to pop someone in the nose. Guess he's been eating his oats and now is feeling them.

Plainfield isn't the only school to name its mascot a Quaker. My alma mater, Wilmington College, has at times called its men's teams Fighting Quakers. Earlham College's teams were once known as the Fighting Quakers; now they're the kinder, gentler Hustlin' Quakers.

Our Quaker college fight songs, though, have a decided pacifistic leaning: "How Can We Keep from Scoring" (to the tune of "How Can We Keep from Singing") is one. Earlham School of Religion, a Quaker theological school, doesn't have a fight song. Instead, it has a passive-resistance song. Such a pacifist-aggressive attitude explains our traditionally poor win-loss records. A team called the Quakers is rarely a powerhouse.

Our pacifist stance is the one thing that many people know about Quakers (besides oats). We historically stand for peace and are against fighting in wars.

The only people we tend to fight with are other Quakers. More about that later. For now, let's consider the words of Daniel Hill, secretary of Peace Association of Friends in America: "I believe there is more thought and attention given to the cause of peace today, both in this country and Europe, than at any former period.... I think we may reasonably hope that this is the beginning of a new era in the history of the world."

Friend Hill said those words in 1870. He was right—but not in the way he thought. We did enter a new era following his words. Since then we have experienced mechanized death and wholesale slaughter of civilians on a scale that neither Hill nor anybody else in 1870 could have imagined.

Which gives me pause. Laboring for peace certainly doesn't seem to have made much difference. And it's hard work. Maybe I'll just give in and slug the next person who annoys me.

Every time I begin to think like that (and relish the idea of punching pesky ATVers—all-terrain vehicle riders—in the snout), I hear this wee little voice that says, "You're called to be faithful." And for me being faithful means being peaceful. I'm pretty sure it's Jesus—though it might be His sidekick on earth, Deborah Fisch, who, in addition to being my boss, is one of my best friends and a really good Friend. I've found that Jesus and Deborah sound a lot alike, probably because she quotes Him so much.

When I hear that wee little voice, I think of what Ron Mock, associate professor of political science and peace studies at George Fox University, said. Mock says that there are three "essential" (though I'd prefer optional!) teachings that are the basis for working for peace today:

1. the belief that we are intended by God to have an eternal loving relationship, even with our enemies.
2. the belief that forgiveness is even more central to relationships than is justice or vengeance.
3. the belief that an omnipotent and loving God will always, without exception, provide a way to give all people means to meet their needs, if we can only find it and follow it.

Oh, really. Really? These three things just don't fit my understanding of how the world works. Perhaps that's part of the problem: the world works in ways different from how God works.

When I look at Mock's first assertion, I think, *Hmmm. I know that Jesus said that we were to love our enemies. But be in "eternal loving relationship" with them? C'mon. I don't even like myself all the time.* So it's hard for me to think that I've gotta love someone I hate. Especially for all eternity.

I guess this idea shows just how amazing grace is. It reminds me of something I need reminding of all the time—that is, as Friend Stephen Grellet said, while "I expect to pass through this world but once," my life has eternal ramifications. I am more than a pudgy, bald, extremely pale-skinned body. I am a soul. Meant for eternity. The same is true for my enemies. Since that's true, I'd better learn to get along with 'em now. May as well start practicing that everlasting love and harmony bit now—"everlasting" is gonna be a long, long time, I suspect.

When I think of Mock's second point, I hear the voice of my sister Kathleen as a kid saying, "But it's not fair." She said that a lot back when she was known as Chatty Kathy. She matched H. L. Mencken's definition of Puritanism—"the haunting fear that *someone, somewhere is having a good time.*" In her case, I think it could have been amended to "the haunting fear that *Brent is somewhere having a good time.*"

That mostly had to do with my having a later bedtime, getting to drive first, and so on. I think back then she was a bit upset she had been born after me. As we all know now, life ain't fair. And neither is God. My perceived need for revenge or what I think is justice is outside of God's nature. God is about love and justice but it's a justice that far supersedes my limited understanding of it. In the way that God forgives me, God wants me to be in the forgiveness business.

No thanks! I don't always want to forgive. Especially those who have wounded me. Personally. Because it is all about me.

It is!

Really.

My daughter Lisa helped me learn that perhaps it's not. And taught me a lesson in forgiveness at the same time. In 1995, Lisa's brother Bruce (Lisa and Bruce are my stepchildren) was murdered. The details don't matter here. What matters is Lisa's response. After the man who killed Bruce was convicted, Lisa found herself on an elevator in the courthouse with the man's family. Lisa screwed up her courage and turned and told them how sad she was that two young men's lives were ruined by this tragedy. And Lisa is not anything if she's not sincere. She meant it.

I was proud of her. I also doubted I could do that. I hope that I could. Forgive us our sins.

For me, Mock's third point shows how powerful, how active, and how...well, how *God* God is. I may say that God is omnipotent and in control. Learning to live peacefully is a way of putting what I say I believe into practical practice.

That's hard. Do I really care about others'—especially my enemies' (or whoever my country says are my enemies)—needs getting met? Or do I just care about my own? Ummmm. And do I really believe that God's providence is enough for all of humankind and the reason there are wars and strife is because we just don't care to find ways to make it available to those in need?

> *Peacemaking is action—love in action.*

I hate those kinds of questions.

Regardless, Mock's teachings call for action. They remind me that Jesus does not call me to passivity. Jesus does not say, "Blessed are the pacifists." Instead He says, "Brent, blessed are the peacemakers. Now get out there and make some peace." Me, Lord? "Yes, Brent. Peacemaking is action—love in action. Haven't you always said that you'd rather be a lover than a fighter? Prove it!"

For me, learning the way of love as a way of life finds its foundation ultimately in my learning to trust God and to remember that "God is not alone the God of things as they are but the God of things as they are meant to be."

Certainly I'm cynical about the possibility of there ever being peace. I'm cynical about a lot of things. Peace is just one of them. I completely got it when my late buddy Alan Garinger came up with a unique idea. "Every town," he said, "has its war memorial. It's about time we had a peace monument."

What made his proposal unique was that it was for a proportional peace monument. That is, its size would be in proportion to the total times of peace humankind has known. "It'll be pretty small," he said with a sigh. He built a full-scale model. It was two inches by two inches by one inch.

He made it out of sugar cubes. That way, when it rained, it would disappear. "Never been a lasting peace anyways," Alan grumbled.

Alan started a campaign to raise a "fund" ("Funds would be too much.") to erect the monument and the bleacher ("No need for bleachers. Who but we Quakers, Mennonites, and Brethren would come?"). He even made bumper stickers—printed on address labels so they'd be in proportion.

Alas, he died before his dream was realized. As he looks down upon us now, I'm sure Alan's thinking, *See? No peace.*

Yet, we need to know peace. If we are children of the God of things as they are meant to be, and followers and friends of Jesus, then we must ask the Spirit for power to live lives of peace. To work for peace. We must try what Love will do in the assurance that, if we do, we will find greater peace in our lives, neighborhoods, and world. Peace, not war, is what God has made us for.

Quick Quaker Questions

Remember, no one right answer. What's your soul say?

- What is the place of peace in my life?
- Do I recognize God as my ultimate source of security?
- What things do I do to help find peace?
- What do I do to create peace?

Unfriendly Persuasion

"Get off my land!" I bellowed. Yes, Mr. Bill bellows. Oh, no! I shouted those words, hands cupped around my mouth, at a bunch of ATVers tearing up and down the creek bed below me. Then, heart racing along with my mouth, I scrambled down the hillside to where they were churning up muddy water, driving up and down the creek bank, and zipping up into the field where I'd freshly planted tree saplings.

I was a teensy upset. Okay, I was steaming! I was so mad that I wished I could have just punched one of 'em. Especially the doofus, um, I mean *child of God* who smiled as he ran over my foot while speeding off. By the time I got back up the hill, I had a really good mad on. Julie and Dave, my youngest sister and her husband, were there when it happened—and love to tell the story of the fire-breathing Quaker pacifist chasing wild riders off his property.

But this isn't about the yahoos who trespass on our property (on horseback, in Jeeps, on foot, with hunting dogs, destroying prairie flowers and grass, trampling trees—"Oh, this is private property? We didn't know"). Nope, it's about me and how, despite my longtime and growing aversion to and abhorrence of war, I'm just not a very peaceful person.

Which is one reason I'm a Quaker today. I need to be. It challenges me. It rubs up against the parts of me that need smoothed out. A lot! The early Quakers said they lived in that spirit that takes away the desire for all war. Which I take to mean all violence. I don't live in that spirit enough. I mean, I'm better than I used to be. But the heart of the killer that was in me as a young kid still resides (at least partially). I often have the feeling, despite my public testimony against violence, that there are some people who just need a good slapping. And I can usually name just who they are!

In the early days of the Association of Bad Friends on Facebook, my Quaker coconspirator Jacob Stone and I came up with a way for me (and others who might share it) to indulge in that feeling. We proposed instituting a series of Quaker indulgences.

The way it would work is that if someone has really ticked you off and you'd just love to smack some sense into him, you could donate five hundred dollars (in addition to your regular giving) to your favorite Friendly organization. In return, the Association of Bad Friends would issue you a one-day indulgence from what we Quakers call our Peace Testimony (a testimony for Quakers is something we collectively witness to. We have testimonies about simplicity, equality, peace, and more). That way you could skip calling your Lutheran brother-in-law and just go bop the offender yourownself.

Well, of course, while Jacob and I thought it was an extremely clever idea, it's not all that helpful. What I want, what I *need*, is to learn to live in that the Spirit that takes away any desire to inflict injury—whether physical, emotional, intellectual, whatever—on another person. I want to know that Spirit who, early Friend James Nayler said,

> delights to do no evil, nor to revenge any wrong, but delights to endure all things, in hope to enjoy its own in the end. Its hope is to outlive all wrath and contention, and to weary out all exaltation and cruelty, or whatever is of a nature contrary to itself. It sees to the end of all temptations. As it bears no evil in itself, so it conceives none in thought to any other. If it be betrayed, it bears it, for its ground and spring is the mercies and forgiveness of God. Its crown is meekness, its life is everlasting love unfeigned.

That speaks to my untamed, unruly, often hateful heart.

QUICK QUAKER QUESTIONS

Remember, no one right answer. What's your soul say?

- Who in my life just needs a good smack? Why do I feel that way about him, her, or them?
- What do I do to remain peaceful when something really annoying happens? Or beyond annoying?
- How would it feel to live in a spirit of repentance, confession, and forgiveness?
- Am I really willing to leave vengeance to God and pray for my enemies?

Stumbles in Bad Quaker History: An Unpeaceable People

In 1828, theological and other tensions got so bad that at the annual gathering of Ohio Quakers, shouting and other nonsilent, nonpeaceful activity led to wrestling, wrangling, furniture smashing, choking, biting, and throwing other Quakers out the windows. The county sheriff had to be dispatched with arrest warrants. Bad Quakers!

Let Us Then Try What Love Will Do

Besides living lives of peace, Quakers are also urged to live simply. We believe a simple life makes peace more possible (more about that later). I'm bad at that, too. Back in the sixties and seventies I was an inveterate hoarder of 45s and LPs, aka "records." In the eighties I began collecting CDs. I'm happy to report all that has changed. I no longer collect records or CDs by the score. Now it's MP3s. And I still have most of the records, CDs, cassettes, 8-tracks, and reel-to-reel tapes that I ever bought or made.

Sigh. Stumble.

The good thing is that all that acquisition hasn't been in vain. Well, much of it has. My wife thinks my Ray Stevens collection dating back to the sixties is silly. It is—but that's the point of Ray Stevens. Songs like "Harry the Hairy Ape" are supposed to be silly. But I've learned a lot from various pieces of music, such as an album I found in the early seventies. On one of my frequent long afternoons in the record department of F. R. Lazarus in downtown Columbus, Ohio, I came across something in the bargain rack. It was a flop in an era of successful spiritual rock songs, most notably Norman Greenbaum's "Spirit in the Sky." The record I found had a cover featuring Edward Hicks's painting the *Peaceable Kingdom* along with two long-haired fellows inserted. Long hair wasn't unusual in those days. Even I had long hair then. What was unusual was that all of the songs had spiritual themes based on Quaker writings. So, I plunked down my $1.49 and took it home.

It really wasn't very good. In fact, I think it was one of the LPs I let my ex-wife have when we divvied up our music collection. But it was the first time I heard the expression "Let us then try what love will do" sung or spoken. It was memorable enough that I was curious where it came from. I found that William Penn said it: "Let us then try what Love will do: for if men did once see we love them, we should soon find they would not harm us. Force may subdue, but Love gains: and he that forgives first, wins the laurel."

Hearing those words was the beginning of a slow journey in learning to live a more peaceful daily life.

What I like about it is that, like all Quaker principles, it is more than just a good idea or philosophy. It is deeply rooted in the teachings of Jesus. It's about not just accepting grace—which I do all the time!—it's about extending grace. To try what love will do is a call to life- and attitude-changing positive action. This appealed to hyperactive me.

Unlike many Christians, I am not attracted to a life of denial and giving up. Oh, I get that those are good things. Even necessary things. For other peo-

> *To try what love will do is a call to life- and attitude-changing positive action.*

ple. Desert fathers and mothers. The saints of the church. You.

I much prefer, though, to do something positive. As kids in church we were often urged to give up sin in the form of things like going to the movies or listening to rock-and-roll music or—horrors—roller skating. Well, that last one was easy. I *hate* roller skating! We were asked to forego our comfortable existences and trek off to Timbuktu. It was always "Give up something." Try as I might, I wasn't good at it. It's a character flaw, I admit. As I've said, I'm bad at being good.

And I could be called again and again and again to quit being hateful or loving violence. But if someone did me wrong (or what I considered wrong), I could get a good mad on and punish the person for days. Just ask my poor first wife. I wasn't pleasant about slights real or perceived. I was trying to put into practice the way of peace. I could do that. Probably because it was more theoretical and removed. But in my daily life, not so much. Hate flared at drivers who cut me off, fellow workers who seemed more favored than I, and so on.

Until I heard that record. Then I began to think, *Have I ever tried to see what Love would do?* Not love but Love. God's Love. What would it be like to treat those around me with Love? All the time. Not in the abstract, but in the day-to-day stuff of life?

For one thing I knew I'd have to start treating those closest to me a bit nicer. I'd have to remember what it was like to be in love with my spouse. I'd have to treat my children with more of the wonder I had on the days I saw them born. I'd have to…oh, the list is just too long to continue here.

For another thing, I'd have to start remembering that it's not all about me. Sigh. Really? I'm not the center of my universe? Shoulder slump. If that's the case, then it just might be that the driver who cut me off was racing to the hospital to tend to someone in dire need. Okay, so that probably wasn't the reason. But it could happen.

I knew I'd have to start small. If I started big, I'd fail big. So I didn't start by trying to be peaceful and loving toward…um, I've forgotten whom I found most annoying at the time. Instead I tried to be more loving to my family—the people I was living with. Sometimes I succeeded. Sometimes I failed. Drastically. That's shown by the fact that I have a former spouse. Major stumble.

While I'm not very good at being peaceful, I want to be. So over the years I've started asking myself a series of tiny queries when I'm feeling especially warlike. I need tiny queries because when I'm heated and smoke is coming out of my ears and eyes, I need quick stops. You might find some of these practices helpful, too.

How Can I Be Helpful?

Even though I'm basically lazy, I start with the hardest question. That's because if I answer this one well, the rest may come easily. And I ask it because it's so against my nature. There are times I'd just really rather be obstructive than helpful. It would be more helpful, for example, to point out to the rampaging ATVers that my side of the creek is a conservation zone whereas the other side of the creek is not, and there are riding trails there, than it would be to scream and foam at the mouth. But if it's not going my way, I may not feel like having it go your way, either. That's why the question helps me—how am I modeling the way of Jesus (which I say I want to do) if I stand in the way of that which benefits someone else?

How Can I Be Caring?

Practicing compassion doesn't cost me anything. Well, actually it does. It's hard to be compassionate and really honked off. So I have to lay down my anger. Which is good, but not as much fun as pouting. But another person's suffering doesn't enhance my standing in this universe. Especially if I contribute to it. Instead, it diminishes me. And my soul's small enough at times.

Am I Really Listening?

As lame as it sounded when the guy rode his horse up the hill into my backyard and said he didn't know it was private property and that he was lost, I could've kept listening. Instead of thinking, *That is so lame! If there are cut trails, no trespassing signs, a barn, a house, how could you not know it was private property?* Listening would have reminded me of my similar mess-ups. Embarrassment (been there myself). Confusion (where am I?!) Self-defensiveness (ooops, as if I've never done that), and more. So what I have to say in response to idiotic—I mean completely normal—statements may not be the most important thing. Especially when there's a chance for disagreement or discord. So I'm learning to listen to what others have to say. Even the idiots. (Yikes, name-calling—another stumble.)

Can I Be Childlike?

Jesus says that the kingdom of heaven (which I imagine to be a true place of peace) is made up of those who are childlike. Honest, trusting, wide-eyed, and noncynical. Powerless. Not easy! Childish is easy for me. Not childlike.

How Am I Going to Be Nonanxious?

Now my friends who know me well have to be snickering at this. Yeah, it's hard to believe that Mr. Anxious (just ask anybody who sits next to me on an airplane!) would say this. Still, it's something I try to think about. Can I hold a situation in prayer and not respond? Can I relax my body and mind and adopt a peaceful posture? Not always, that's for certain. I blow it a lot. But it's a good question and a better practice. It's amazing how it brings peace into a situation. At least peace for me.

Can I Give Up Control?

Actually, I'm not giving up anything but the illusion of control. The reality is that nobody likes to be controlled. I know I don't! So I have to give the annoyers and the situation over to God and trust God to do what is best

Am I Looking for That of God in Them?

Every human is a part of the family of God. Everyone. You say, "Oh, c'mon—even her?" Yes. And if I truly believe that, then I can look for that which unites us—not that which divides us. I mean, who wants to smack his brother or sister? Okay, bad example. But look for that of God in the person you're annoyed with—or is your enemy. You may have to look really hard, but do it.

According to Jesus, there are only two commandments: "Brent, love the Lord your God with all your heart and with all your soul and with all your mind. This is the first and greatest commandment. Listen up, Brent, the second is like it: Love your neighbor as yourself. All the law and the prophets hang on these two commandments" (Matthew 22:37–40 NBBV).

Okay, Jesus, I get it. I am not loving God or my neighbor if I am not being peace-full.

Now maybe I am just a fool. I have often been wrong in my life. But I endeavor to follow the way of Jesus. And to try what Love will do. I'd rather it be said of me, "He lived in love" than "He was right." Well, most of the time. That's because a verse that comes to mean more and more to me as I grow in God (at least I hope I am!) is Micah 6:8.

> He has told you, human one,
>> what is good and
>> what the LORD requires from you:
>>> to do justice, embrace faithful love,
>>> and walk humbly with your God.

I'm not as good as I should be at those things. But I do know that I cannot walk humbly when I am so certain about who my enemies are or what should happen to them—globally, locally, or next door to me. Others may be able to do that. I can't. I've been a long time learning that lesson. I've finally come to see that such hatred and lack of peace damages me more than my supposed enemies. So I'm trying more to tend my soul's garden. Maybe then I might grow the fruits that point people to the God Who Loves Them More Than They Know. I hope someday to grow into a winsome invitation to Christlikeness.

As I find myself more aware of the grace that's been extended to me, I try to extend it to others and let God be in control. "All shall be well, and all shall be well and all manner of things shall be well."

QUICK QUAKER QUESTIONS

Remember, no one right answer. What's your soul say?

- How can I confront violence with peace—even when my personal relationships are concerned?
- Is being peaceful the same as being a doormat?
- Can I steep myself in God's eternal peace and *shalom* so that it becomes part of my nature?

If I am called to be a friend of all humankind and to proclaim peace upon the earth in Jesus' name, then I have to remember that being a peacemaker doesn't mean that I won't get hit. It just means that *I* won't be the one doing the hitting. Which is important.

Again, peacemaking in the way of Jesus is not about being passive, a doormat, a victim. It is actively resisting abusive power and not cooperating with it. Which means I run the risk of getting smacked—or worse. I may suffer. But my suffering is better than my passing on the violence to others.

For me, it also means—and this is really hard for me—that my words and thoughts, to whatever extent that I can (with Divine assistance), will be nonviolent. I have to walk so close to Jesus that I refuse to name-call, accuse, belittle, intimidate, or demonize the "enemy"—be it ISIS or some other terrorist group or my spouse when I'm just in a grumpy mood.

Am I perfectly at peace? Nope. But as Friend Sydney Bailey said,

"Peace begins within ourselves. It is to be implemented within the family, in our meetings, in our work and leisure, in our own localities, and internationally. The task will never be done. Peace is a process to engage in, not a goal to be reached."

"The task will never be done." Indeed.

CHAPTER 3

TO BUY OR NOT TO BUY

Living Simply When I'd Really Like a New Mercedes—Or Even a Honda!

Simplicity is the name we give to our effort to free ourselves to give full attention to God's still, small voice: the sum of our efforts to subtract from our lives everything that competes with God for our attention and clear hearing.
—Lloyd Lee Wilson

Living simply is the right ordering of our lives and priorities.
—Leonard Kenworthy

Therefore, I say to you, don't worry about your life, what you'll eat or what you'll drink, or about your body, what you'll wear. Isn't life more than food and the body more than clothes?
—Jesus

Progress is man's ability to complicate simplicity.
—Thor Heyerdahl

43

'Tis the gift to be simple, 'tis the gift to be free
'Tis the gift to come down where we ought to be,
And when we find ourselves in the place just right,
'Twill be in the valley of love and delight.
When true simplicity is gained,
To bow and to bend we shan't be ashamed,
To turn, turn will be our delight,
Till by turning, turning we come 'round right.
—*Shaker Elder Joseph Brackett*

I'm not certain I'm gaining on simplicity. Sometimes it seems closer. Sometimes it seems farther away. After all, I've already admitted that I'm a music hoarder. I also horde books: floor to ceiling in my office, filled shelves in the loft, random books lying all over the house on end tables and nightstands and on kitchen shelves, boxes of books in the basement and garage attic. And I don't just mean copies of books I've written in attempts to make me a best seller. I mean books by other people.

That's why I was a bit disconcerted to pick up my Bible and read this:

> And he told them this parable: "The house of a certain rich man yielded an abundant harvest of books. He thought to himself, 'What shall I do? I have no place to store my books.'
>
> "Then he said, 'This is what I'll do. I will hire a contractor to come and build new bookshelves in the loft and in the living room, and in them I will store many of my books. The rest I will put in boxes in the garage attic until I can build more bookshelves. And I'll say to myself, 'You have plenty of books laid up for many years. Take life easy; eat, drink, and read on.'
>
> "But God said to him, 'You fool! This very night your life will be demanded from you. Then who will get what you have prepared for yourself— including the author-autographed first editions?'" (Luke 12:16–20 NBBV)

Yikes! What's God got against books? I'm sure glad Jesus didn't say anything about garages or barns. My barn is full and I should have built a bigger one. There's my car. Nancy's car. The farm pickup. My antique MG. There's a utility tractor with a loader, rotary mower, log splitter, box scraper, grading blade, and more. A lawn tractor. A high-speed, zero-turn mower. A push mower. A utility golf cart with a dump bed. Various trimmers, rakes, shovels, hoes, pitchforks, saws, chain saws, and so on. People hear I live on a farm and say, "Man, I'd love to live the simple life." Lemme tell you, it ain't so simple—otherwise I wouldn't need all this equipment. And I do need it!

Or do I?

This is something I've been learning about—or at least struggling with—on the topic of simplicity over the years: there is no one way to live simply. I wish there were. It would make my life easier—at least I would know exactly how badly I'm failing at it!

I once heard someone say, "One person's simplicity may be another person's complexity." Indeed. I could go all Walden and live in a tiny cabin in the woods. But I doubt our big family would appreciate that. Besides, Henry David Thoreau could stand it for only a couple of years. I do know a Friend who did it for five years. Mark Burch, who's written some really good stuff on simplicity (see the appendices), lived in the Canadian woods in a simple hut. "When my parents came for their first visit," he said in a talk to Quakers about simplicity, "my mother cried."

> *Being cumbered is how the things we own end up owning us.*

Mark lived this simple life in the woods and found that, while he was indeed living simply, it was not filled with lots of time for personal reflections that could be turned into a best-selling classic of literature like *Walden* or *Life in the Woods*. Life in the woods was just too

45

demanding! Physically and mentally. He was bone- and mind-weary. As he said in that same speech, "I was cumbered with all that it took to live simply that way." "Cumbered" is how early Quakers referred to the way the things we own (or think we own) weigh us down and steal attention away from the life of the Spirit. Being cumbered is how the things we own end up owning us. Which is why I need to build more bookshelves and a bigger barn. Stumble.

True simplicity is not about how little I have (though some Friends do live very, very modestly) or how much you have. Rather it's about why we have what we have.

While that may sound like a bad Quaker's way of rationalizing how much stuff he has, it's true. Which flies in the face of much of what I was taught about simplicity. Didn't Jesus tell the rich young ruler that, to inherit eternal life, he needed to sell all he had?

He sure did. So I should sell everything I have?

Well, yeah, if Jesus was talking to me when he said it. I'm not certain that he was. I'm pretty certain that he was talking to *you* about that. Not me so much.

Seriously, scriptures like that feel pretty guilty trippy. I let faith guilt me in other ways, too. Our little Quaker meeting is filled (well, as *filled* as a group of thirty can be) with people who travel all around the world doing good things: Kenya. Belize. Palestine. Cuba. These good people host visitors from those countries who need a place to stay when they come here. Invariably we first-worlders start talking about how rich we are compared to those from developing nations.

We are. There's no denying that.

Okay, if Jesus said to get rid of everything and I'm so much richer than the Kenyans I know, maybe I should sell all I possess and give to the poor. But like the rich young ruler, I'd probably go away distressed and grieving, for like him, I own much property.

So if living simply for me consists of a Walden-like existence, subsisting on the bare minimum, I've got a long way to go and much to learn. And I probably am not going to make it.

What's a fella (or woman or family or faith community) to do if he wants to "come 'round right"? First, I have to start with recognizing that the right kind of simplicity is not about masochism or negative denial. It is not, "This'll hurt but will be good for you." I hear that enough from my doctor! I don't need to hear it from my church. Instead, I need help in learning to live fully with the things I need, moving past the many things our consumer society says I need, and being a radical witness to the good life in this day. Simplicity is about saying to myself (and to the world at large) that we can live for more than mere acquisition.

If I die with the most toys, I don't win. I'm as dead as the poorest beggar on the street. I win when I am unencumbered by stuff and fully the friend of Jesus. That kind of simplicity gives me freedom.

QUICK QUAKER QUESTIONS

Remember, no one right answer. What's your soul say?

- What feelings come to mind when I first think about living simply? Honestly?
- Are they good? Or uncomfortable? Or "No way, I'm not eating bean sprouts and living in a tent"?

Stumbles in Bad Quaker History: He Must Have Missed "Simplicity Sunday"

On June 21, 1933, John Dillinger, the son of a Quaker elder and one of the few people ever known to be expelled from a Quaker Sunday school class, robbed his first of twelve banks.

QUAKER? LIKE THE AMISH, RIGHT?

When some people find out that I'm a Quaker, they begin looking around for my horse and buggy. Why people think we're Amish is beyond me. Well, not really. All many people know about Quakers is the guy on the oats box. He looks sorta Amish. Until you look closely. Then you see he's not dressed anything like the Amish—way too stylin' for them.

Two hundred years ago, the Quakers did kinda dress like the Amish. And we used horses and buggies. But so did everyone else, as Henry Ford still hadn't come up with the Model T (which came only in the Quakers' favorite color—black!). We also didn't use electricity— like the Amish. But that's only because Thomas Edison hadn't figured out how to get electricity into our houses so we could stop watching television by candlelight. Quakers, though, unlike the Amish, have kept up with the times. While the Amish live totally off the grid as a testimony to God and as a spiritual discipline of simplicity, we Quakers have moved into the twentieth century. Some of us have even moved into the twenty-first. And we've brought our testimony of simplicity with us.

Simplicity has been a part of our faith almost since we began. Sometimes we've done it very well. Sometimes, not so well (remember John Dillinger?). Early Quakers spoke and dressed "plain." For them, plain language meant calling the days of the week by numbers instead of their common names—First Day for Sunday, for example—as a way to avoid pagan influences (Thor for Thursday!). They did that with months, too, since they had incorrect names (December was no longer the tenth month). They wore simple clothes in basic colors as a witness against the fancy dress and classism of their day. They wouldn't doff their hats or bow down to their social superiors, either.

The not-so-well came in when we allowed these things to become a badge of distinction—setting ourselves apart in a way that drew attention to us as a non-humble people. Even from the start, some wise Friends thought dressing plain was a bit much—an affectation that didn't do any good except make us stranger than we already were. Margaret Fell, who married George Fox, once wrote:

> But Christ Jesus said: that we must take no thought what we shall eat, or what we shall drink, or what we shall put on: but tells to us consider, the lilies how they grow in more royalty than Solomon, Matt. 6:28-31. Instead contrary to this we must look at no colors, nor make anything that is changeable colors as the hills are, nor sell them, nor wear them. But we must be all in one dress, and one color. This is a silly poor gospel. It is more fit for us, to be covered with God's eternal Spirit, and clothed with his eternal Light which leads us, and guides us into righteousness, and to live righteously and justly and holy in this profane evil world. This is the clothing that God puts upon us, and likes, and will bless.

A silly poor gospel, indeed. So silly were our dress and habits that they even made us the brunt of cartoons! One portrays a snooty look-ing, plain-dressed Quaker chap walking down the street as a smirking scamp mockingly bows down to him—since the Quakers wouldn't bow to anybody, believing as we do that all humans are equal before God. Even royalty. That stance often made us look uppity. And maybe, just maybe, some of us were.

But one thing about us Quakers is that the way we live our faith is evolving. We believe that God always has something to teach us about being people of faith in our current times. So we ask lots of questions hoping to find out how to live godly lives. Or looking for loopholes. (Is stealing still against God's will? Appears so.)

The issue of simplicity in a modern, consumerist society is one of the things that keeps us growing spiritually. At least it does me. Because I'm not good at this simplicity bit.

The bad news—for you—is that what it means for me is not what it'll necessarily mean for you. The good news for you is that my way of living simply may not be your way. What? How can this be both bad and good news?

It's bad because you can just say, "Oh, here's how Brent does it. I'll do that, too." Nope. Won't work. My way is not your way. Or vice versa. So don't be looking in this book for some exact model for living simply. You won't find it.

It's good because our faith is not one-size-fits-all. At least in how we live it out. We are each unique—and created by God to be so. Which means, when Paul says (Philippians 2:12) we have to work out our salvation with fear and trembling, I think he should have added something such as "and likewise about living it out!" Each of us needs to work out what it means to live simply.

For me, simplicity is often a matter of a faithful attitude—or trying to have one, at least. Why do I have stuff? I didn't grow up the richest kid on the block—or even the third richest. So when I had my first allowances and then summer jobs, I bought stuff I *wanted* (much to the dismay of my dad, who wanted me to buy stuff I needed, like shoes and jeans). I acquired because I could. That was a pattern of living that continued for many years. Stumble.

While that still occasionally occurs, usually I buy now because I need something. Other times I buy something I need but that also makes a statement about my values.

The first is the easiest to understand, I suppose. It takes a lot of stuff to live simply on fifty acres. Seriously. If, that is, a person is trying to plant tallgrass prairie or reforest acres of hardwood trees. Yes, I could leave it all alone and let nature take its course. Then I wouldn't need most of the equipment I have. But then this land would become a hodgepodge of invasive plant species, non-native grasses, and briar. It takes a lot of work to restore the handiwork of humankind to something more in keeping with what this land was like two hundred years ago. Which is the stewardship to which I've been called. Though after some really long days out in the prairie I sure wish I hadn't been!

The second is perhaps harder to understand. I lived years without even thinking about it. But I realize now that what I own says a lot about what I believe. Or value.

Awareness of my slow evolution in this came on a trip to Texas a few years ago. My sister Kathleen and her husband, Paul, lived there then. I stayed with them when I was on a speaking tour for one of my books. A book in which I talked some about Quaker simplicity. I flew in and needed to borrow one of Paul and Kathleen's cars to get to my speaking gig at the Catholic Campus Ministry Center at Southern Methodist University. My choice was between their Mercedes and their BMW.

Yikes. Sigh. I love cars. I admit it. Especially foreign cars. Especially British or European cars. I've owned a couple (the MG I still have, an Austin-Healey Sprite in my early twenties, various Volkswagens, and...well, too many cars to mention). I've dreamt of owning a classic Jaguar saloon (a "saloon" sounds classier than a "four-door sedan," doesn't it?) with wood dash, leather seats, and pop-up picnic tables affixed to the back of the front seats. I would have made do with a Mercedes or BMW, but a big Jag was my dream car. Once I had it made financially, one was going to be in my garage.

Now I'm gonna say right here that I still love Jags. But a few years back I decided I wouldn't plan to own one anymore. I could afford one. I just couldn't *buy* one. Simplicity was the reason. I realized that my possessions said something about what I believed. I didn't want to hear people thinking, *Oh, he says he's about the simple life, but did you see that expensive car he's driving?* My driving a Jag, and people's comments (spoken or not) would have shifted everything away from my feeble attempts to live faithfully to "Look how badly he's doing at that!"

I mean, though I've already admitted to being a bad Friend, I don't want to confirm it in others' eyes by the kind of car I'm driving.

A Jaguar, to me, says *wealth, class,* and *elegance.* There is nothing wrong with any of those per se. I was delighted that Kathleen and Paul could enjoy such fine automobiles. But for me to own one would play into my own weaknesses regarding those things—especially wealth and class (and the classism and privilege that they can engender and/or maintain in me). The weird thing is I don't really feel deprived by not driving a Jag. The Buick I have now is better built, better engineered, has more bells and whistles than the first Jaguar 420 I contemplated buying in 1971.

It doesn't have those picnic tables, though!

And so I felt really awkward about driving either of those cars. What would it say to the students about Quakers and our values (including simplicity) to have their guest speaker arrive driving a BMW or a Benz?

I chose the Benz.

And enjoyed it immensely.

It was black.

Simply Quakerly.

And I parked two blocks away.

QUICK QUAKER QUESTIONS

Remember, no one right answer. What's your soul say?

- What do the things I own say about my beliefs or values?
- Do I keep my life uncluttered by things?
- How could I center my daily life in God so that all things (including possessions) take their rightful place?

Stumbles in Bad Quaker History: Vanity, Vanity, All Is Vanity Plates

In the early 1980s, while working for Quakers in Indiana, I pulled into a meeting's parking lot and parked next to a very nice car. Okay, it was a luxury model. Luxuriant model, even. As I walked behind it, I noticed it had a personalized license plate. "Quaker" it proclaimed. Those plain-dressing Friends "sleeping" out in the cemetery must have been so proud.

STEWARDSHIP

I've always hated Stewardship Sunday at church. Someone was always trying to guilt me in to giving more money away than I wanted to. Yeah, there was the usual disclaimer that stewardship was about more than money. But I knew it wasn't.

Then I heard someone say that stewardship meant an "activity or job of protecting and being responsible for something."

Really? It's not just a five-dollar word that meant give another five (or five hundred) dollars to the church? If that's the case, then maybe it's a better word than I've given it credit for. Part of my conversion is due in no small part to the fact that I am shocked to find myself living on a fifty-acre farm in Indiana. I planned on living in a condominium downtown in some big city. But for the past whole lotta years I've been living in a house nestled against the woods overlooking the West Branch of White Lick Creek.

This is not a piece of land I'd scraped and saved for. Nope. Nancy's a farm girl and this land was some of her family's property. It came to us as part of her inheritance, albeit a bit before her father's passing. And it has taught me more than a few lessons in stewardship and how it relates to simplicity.

The first was in what kind of house to build. What could we do in building that expressed our Quaker faith? As I said earlier, the Quaker understandings of peace, simplicity, and care for the earth are all part of the gospel as we understand it. We lived that in new ways as we were faced with how and what to build and my own new understanding of how what I owned spoke loudly about what I believed.

A few years earlier we'd fallen in love with our friends' post-and-beam house. Phil and Esther had built one of the first Yankee Barn Homes in Indiana. When we found out that the home used timbers reclaimed from old factories and the like, was superinsulated and energy efficient, we were sold. Even a bad Quaker like me gets the wisdom of such building—it would save me tons of money in energy costs. So we designed a place that was open for hosting groups, with guest rooms for travelers that used geothermal heating and cooling, and which could accommodate us as we aged—wide doorways through which a wheelchair would fit and a one-level floor plan for us (other levels for grandkids, guests, caregivers).

It was not inexpensive.

This was hard for me—for as bad as I am, I do think about such things. Yet, given my income at the time, our levels of giving, and so forth, it was the right thing to do. For one, our footprint on the ecology was going to be lower than a traditional, though less-expensive-to-build, stick-built home. For another, it would last a long time and be the last home we needed to have.

Besides, I told myself, a house like this sitting on fifty acres would be a gold mine when we decided to sell it. It's on one of the last undeveloped sections of our county. Richness, here we come.

Then something weird happened to me. I was God-smacked. That happens to me a lot. Subtle messages don't get my attention, so God allowed something to happen that would. I was asked to serve on the storm water commission for our county. This was at the time I began seeing major erosion along the banks of our little creek. It was becoming a big creek. And then beginning to flood. And washing my land and new trees downstream. *My* land. *My* trees.

This was at the same time that I had started seeing the occasional deer and raccoon and beaver. These were all critters repopulating land that had been over-herbicided and -pesticided and left nothing for them to feed on—crickets, butterflies, wildflowers. They—and more, including mink and fox and wild turkeys—had once been plentiful on this plot of earth.

I liked seeing the wildlife. I didn't like seeing the erosion. The erosion, I learned, was coming from all the overdevelopment in our country. The subdivisions of new big houses. The warehouses filled with goods. Shopping centers so we could go buy those goods.

My dreams of big money from some land developer began to fade. I decided for the deer and other critters and against a big-box retailer.

Where had those new values come from? Thanks a lot, eighteenth-century Quaker John Woolman and Jesus. Sigh.

Now I found myself pondering big questions. *How do I care for this land? What's God want me to do with it? Do I have to do what God wants?* I don't like big questions. I like small, simple ones—what do you want for dinner, does this tie go with this shirt, Mary Ann or Ginger?

I was living in a house based on my Quaker values. We'd called it Ploughshares Farm because the beams came from former armament factories and we wanted it to be a place of peace ("And they shall beat their swords into plowshares"). Wasn't that enough?

Evidently not. As I wrestled with the ideas of simplicity and care for the earth, I began pondering what it meant for me to "own" this land.

Which took me to the new idea (for me) of stewardship. Protecting. Being Responsible. We had been given this land. And the house (yes, we had paid for the house, but it felt like a gift). A shopping center or grocery store or even a gravel pit didn't seem like protecting or being responsible. It certainly didn't feel like living up to a notion of a simple lifestyle. The more I pondered, the more I watched the hundred-dollar bills take wing like redwing blackbirds in the field I was contemplating selling some future day. I knew that land development was not what I was called to do. Sigh.

So I contacted various county, state, and federal agencies. Together we drew up plans. Our family began planting fruit and nut bushes and trees for wildlife. We put in almost ten acres of tallgrass prairie. We planted thousands of Indiana hardwoods. I learned to drive a tractor, operate chain saws, split wood, make trails, and a whole buncha stuff that still surprises me. The biggest surprise is that I've become, if not one with, at least part of the land. This is home. And the place where I've lived the longest.

Tending this land feels like a spiritual calling. Though I could really do without the mosquitoes, biting flies, ticks, and poison ivy.

We've paid down our debt. I've moved to a less-demanding (and poorer-paying!) job. I have more time to work the land when it needs work. I have more time to write when the land is resting. We're living more frugally, in spite of all the equipment it takes to run the place. We welcome lots of travelers to the farm. And a worship group met here on Sunday evenings for more than seven years.

It's been complex learning to live simply.

It's been complex learning to live simply. I've described what it means for me. It may mean something completely different for you. I'd be surprised if it doesn't. If not, there are thirty acres for sale right next door!

QUICK QUAKER QUESTIONS

Remember, no one right answer. What's your soul say?

- What do I do to keep my life uncluttered by things and activities?
- What daily life conditions overwhelm me?
- Do I have something that I'm responsible for protecting?
- How may my habits and addictions be caused by things such as media, social expectations, or personal shortcomings? (Ouch.)

TOOLS OF UNIVERSAL LOVE

So I find myself with all this land and stuff. Besides use it and enjoy it—a high-speed mower quits being fun after the third mowing of the season!—what else am I supposed to do with it? John Woolman says the business of our lives is to "turn all the treasures we possess into the channel of universal love."

Woolman, unlike me, was a good Quaker. He worked valiantly and humbly against slave holding. He began wearing undyed, plain clothes since the dye was produced by slave labor. He was a ray of white in a sea of Quaker black and grey—and was thought odd for it. He worked part-time so that he was free to travel in ministry and witness. He lived his faith and his actions matched his words. He was considered a bit of an odd duck in the Friendly pond at the time.

His words, when I first encountered them as young man, didn't have much impact. I thought they would make a good—if long— bumper sticker. But how can that be practical, to turn all we own into a channel of universal love? I can turn some things I own into specific love: I give books to my friends not expecting their return. I loan my pickup truck to people who need to haul things. We open our house to visiting travelers. I . . .

Oh wait. That's one way it's done! By holding loosely to the things we have. Realizing that they are things—not possessions.

This is a hard lesson for me. I mean, I'll loan the truck. It's just a truck—albeit pretty new and low-mileage. But it's insured. It gets crashed, it gets fixed. The 1955 MG—hmmm, I have to think more about that. I think of it as more than just a car—it's family history. The fellow I was named for, Brent Stephens, bought it new in 1955. I rode in it as a little kid. After he parked it and didn't drive it for years, my dad, John, whom I'm also named for, convinced Brent to sell it to him in the late sixties. I drove it as a teenager and young college student. We have family pictures of all of us kids in it. And our kids in it. And friends in it. My grandkids in it. And it being driven in all kinds of cool places (like on the Indianapolis Motor Speedway track). So this antique car with less than thirty thousand miles on it has a lot of meaning. Can I loan it as freely?

I'm getting there. It's not always easy. It's easier if, as I said, I focus on a particular love. Would I give a book to Stephanie? Music to Eric? A place to stay to Rick and Jo? Sure thing. Would I give money to a panhandler in Philly? Hmmm. Would I give my wallet—willingly—to someone robbing me? Universal love—God's Love—is harder, especially toward one I don't love, don't know, consider my enemy, or considers me the enemy.

> *How can I sow seeds of peace, instead of war, through what I buy?*

And yet Woolman makes no distinctions like that. Nor does Jesus. Indeed, when we read the entire section from which Woolman's quote was taken, we see that it echoes Jesus' radical commandments to love without reservation and hesitation.

> Our gracious Creator cares and provides for all His creatures; His tender mercies are over all His works, and so far as true love influences our minds, so far we become interested in His workmanship, and feel a desire to make use of every opportunity to lessen the distresses of the afflicted, and to increase the happiness of the creation. Here we have a prospect of one common interest from which our own is inseparable, so that to turn all we possess into the channel of universal love becomes the business of our lives.

"So far as true love influences our minds" we will, at every opportunity, "feel a desire to lessen the distresses of the afflicted." Well, I'm working on that.

And yes, you may borrow my pick-em-up truck.

I still have to think about the MG.

QUICK QUAKER QUESTIONS

Remember, no one right answer. What's your soul say?

- Am I living a life that nurtures an environment that sustains and enriches life for all?
- How can I be more thoughtful about what I need and what I acquire?
- Do I choose with care the use of technology and devices that truly simplify and add quality to my life?
- Do I share my possessions with those who could benefit from them?

THE SEEDS OF WAR

"May we look upon our treasures, and the furniture of our houses, and the garments in which we array ourselves, and try whether the seeds of war have nourishment in these our possessions, or not."

That's another thing John Woolman said. I mean, gimme a break, John. Between him and Jesus I get a lot of challenges to my bad behavior. Woolman wrote this in his "Plea for the Poor." Hmmm, didn't Jesus already make a plea or two for the poor? (Of course, He also said we'd always have poor with us, in a way that seems a little dismissive.) But John, really, how could the seeds of war find food in the things I own—my clothes, my furniture, my cell phone? My cell phone? You're kiddin' me!

Nope. Turns out the seeds of war are in there. Yeah, I knew my iPhone was made in China—probably under conditions that Woolman (or even my ownbadself) would not approve. But there's something in my phone (and your phone and every other electronic device you use). It's called *coltan.*

Never heard of it, eh? Neither had I, until recently. Coltan is short for columbite-tantalite and is used in tantalum capacitors, which allow our phones and other gadgets to get smaller and smaller. Coltan is mined by people living in primitive, often slavelike, conditions, which is bad enough. What's worse is that some of the places it's mined are beset by murder, rape, violence, and abuse on an unimaginable scale in civil wars conducted in no small part by warlords who want to corner the coltan market and make tons of money. In the Democratic Republic of Congo (DRC), for example, aid groups estimate that over five million people have died since 1998, mostly from disease and malnutrition. It is estimated that the DRC has 64 percent or more of the world's supply of coltan—so the rapes, killings, and enslavement are not going to get any better.

All because I want a lighter, faster, smaller telephone/camera/gaming device/status checker gadget to carry around. One I didn't even know I needed a few years ago.

Hmmm, I wonder what other seeds I'm unknowingly nourishing.

Now I didn't tell you about coltan to guilt you into getting rid of your cell phone. Any more than I will get rid of mine. But I'm not going to try to justify having it because of all the work I do on it. Instead, I just want to point out the wisdom of Woolman's advice to look at what we own and see if it comes by ill-gotten means—even if we paid full retail.

How can I sow seeds of peace, instead of war, through what I buy? Some ways are obvious. Purchasing fair-trade goods is one. Fair trade is a movement urging consumers to purchase goods from organizations and companies who help workers achieve a more balanced and fair lifestyle based on fair wages paid for goods made. It is also about sustainability. Fair-trade sellers pay higher prices to exporters and produce (primarily in developing countries) all sorts of things—foods, clothing, crafts, and so on.

Another way is to buy local. Chances are the stuff I buy at the local farmers' market downtown (or that farmstand out in the country) is relatively war-seed free.

Investing in socially responsible funds is another way to avoid those seeds.

Now I've got to go ... my iPhone's ringing.

A CONCLUDING WORD ... OR FEW HUNDRED

Another form of simplicity is less about possession than it is about scheduling. Sometimes I get so busy, even doing God's work, that the center of my life is more cluttered than my barn. What difference does it make if I go live in a plain house with few possessions and drive a plain black Prius if I don't have simplicity in my soul? I have all sorts of "invisible" possessions that appear altruistic to others. But the committee chairmanships, community activities, and so on are things I own (or that own me) and wear as sort of a badge of pride. I must be important—look at how busy (and tired!) I am.

So, if I am ever going to live simply, I have to begin by converging my inner and outer lives. I have to learn to live in a holy center. I have to calm down and breathe. I have to say no to things that merely stroke my ego.

It's not easy. I have a terribly difficult time doing it. It is much easier to run, run, run than it is to sit and listen to God. But when I run, run, run I find my whole life coming unbalanced—family time, work productivity, emotions, physical health. It is when I take time to pray and wait that I find my rhythms, inner and outer, beginning to slow and becoming more soothing than rock-and-roll ragged.

So that's where I must begin—inside. This bad Quaker needs to take time to be holy. When I do so, I find that a holy simplicity follows.

Even more remarkably, with that simplicity comes joy. I know, in my innermost life and mind, that things do not bring me happiness. But I have been a bit slower to learn the lesson that activity, even religious activity, does not bring happiness either. What brings joy into my life is when I give up, abandon myself to God, and allow the Spirit to simplify my life and direct my actions.

That means I must surrender self.

That's not just gonna happen. At least not easily. I would much rather be in control, or fool myself into thinking that I am, of my life than turn it over to anyone else—even God. That's one reason I hate flying (according to a therapist I had. As if I needed to spend a bunch of money to find out I'm a control freak!). I have to sit there and let someone else control my destiny. Somebody I don't know. Somebody who may be having a really bad day.

So I don't trust the pilot. The larger question is do I trust God? Do I trust enough to let go—even when I feel that life will go careening out of control and I may crash upon its rocks? Oftentimes the answer is no. And there is fulfillment, however spiritually unhealthy, in all the activity I work so hard to keep up.

Van Morrison has a song titled "When Will I Ever Learn to Live in God?" That question is mine, too. It is at the heart of my learning to live simply.

Jesus says,

> So, Brent, do not worry, saying, "What shall I eat?" or "What shall I drink?" or "What shall I wear?" For you run after all these things, and your heavenly Father knows that you need them. C'mon Brent, seek first His kingdom and His righteousness, and all these things will be given to you as well. (Matthew 6:31–33 NBBV)

In listing those things I'm not supposed to worry about, Jesus cuts directly to the chase. He points out the things that consume me. He is also saying that I worry too much about the inconsequential. Jesus says if I seek first His kingdom, that is, surrender my idea of what I am to be about to the larger ideas that God has for me, then all the important things will be mine as a matter of course. If I ever learn to simplify my life by surrendering to God, then I'll find I have all I need. Even when it is not all I want.

Again, context is important. Jesus didn't address these words to starving children or displaced homeless ones. He was talking to "good" religious people—like me. Says Henry van Etten:

> It is easy to let ourselves slip into action for action's sake, without noticing it, we unconsciously seek to enlarge our sphere of activity… unconsciously neglecting day after day to restore our spiritual strength, with nothing but our wretched little human powers. Yet we had begun our work…with the highest motives, we even had the intimate sense of response to the divine call; yes, it was with a following wind that we launched out, God filling the sails, and Christ at the helm.
>
> Even so, bit by bit, we have transformed what was a divinely appointed task into work on a merely human level, with all its shortcomings. And why did things end up like that? Because we neglected our inner life, because we were taken up with action, because we were too tired to pray, too tired to take part in meetings for worship, too tired to refresh our spiritual strength by reading…We must be able to stop in the midst of our urgent task for something even more urgent; prayer, self-composure, meditation in silence, worship.

Quick Quaker Questions

Remember, no one right answer. What's your soul say?

- Do I spend my time in ways that reflect my values?
- How do I make sure I take time for personal renewal?
- Can I say no? Do I even know when to say no to things I can't possibly get finished in time or do well?

For me, the practice of simplicity begins with an ordered inner life. This is not a life that is poor and bare, destitute of joy and beauty. Simplicity opens me to all there is to celebrate and welcome into my life—not just the acquisitions I bring into it. When I live an ordered life from the Divine Center, the superfluous details vanish. I experience a simplicity that makes for beauty.

Remember the Shakers' song that opens this chapter? "'Tis the gift to be simple, 'Tis the gift to be free." May I ask God every day for the gift of inner simplicity. In that way, I'll live fully into a life of freedom and beauty.

CHAPTER 4

RED AND YELLOW, BLACK AND WHITE, THEY ARE PRECIOUS IN HIS SIGHT

Um, Perhaps My Vision Needs Checking

Guided by the Light of God within us and recognizing that of God in others, we can all learn to value our differences in age, sex, physique, race and culture.... Jesus stressed the unique nature and worth of each individual.... Personality, sex, race, culture and experience are God's gifts. We need one another and differences shared become enrichments, not reasons to be afraid, to dominate or condemn.

—Meg Maslin

My activism did not spring from my being gay, or, for that matter, from my being black. Rather, it is rooted fundamentally in my Quaker upbringing and the values that were instilled in me by my grandparents who reared me.

—Bayard Rustin

Answering that of God in everyone....

—George Fox

A man went down from Jerusalem to Jericho. He encountered thieves, who stripped him naked, beat him up, and left him near death. Now it just so happened that a priest was also going down the same road. When he saw the injured man, he crossed over to the other side of the road and went on his way. Likewise, a Levite came by that spot, saw the injured man, and crossed over to the other side of the road and went on his way. A Samaritan, who was on a journey, came to where the man was. But when he saw him, he was moved with compassion. The Samaritan went to him and bandaged his wounds, tending them with oil and wine. Then he placed the wounded man on his own donkey, took him to an inn, and took care of him. The next day, he took two full days' worth of wages and gave them to the innkeeper. He said, "Take care of him, and when I return, I will pay you back for any additional costs." What do you think? Which one of these three was a neighbor to the man who encountered thieves?

—*Jesus*

There is nothing more dangerous than the conscience of a bigot.
—*George Bernard Shaw*

"The that of God in me is really having a hard time seeing the that of God in thee today." I said that once to a Quaker whom I was finding more than a little bit annoying. And I've thought it many more times than I've said it aloud. "That of God in everyone" is one of those quirky Quaker concepts based in scripture. John 1:9 specifically: "The true light that shines on all people was coming into the world." "All people" being the operative words. "Red and yellow, black and white" as the old children's Sunday school song says. Also straight, gay, man, woman, trans, boy, girl, Christian, Jew, Muslim, atheist, and so on. It's part of the gospel, not some clunky add-on or twenty-first-century politically correct concept.

As radical Friends of Jesus, the early Quakers took that idea as a literal truth. If I'm enlightened by the light of Christ and the Bible says that everyone else is, too, then I'd better start looking at them with enlightened eyes. Sounds simple. But it's difficult. Sometimes I have a hard time recognizing that of God in myself—let alone in someone who jumped in front of me in the boarding line of a flight. You know, the important things of life!

And yet that's what George Fox, one the first Friends, told us to do—to answer that of God in everyone. Actually he said we were to "walk cheerfully over the earth answering that of God in everyone."

Cheerfully? Wonder if he and Jesus would settle for grudgingly answering that of God in everyone?

Nah, probably not.

Which is why I had to change my attitude recently when someone wanted to come for a visit. "I'd like to get to know you better," he said. Well, I had been out mowing and running a line trimmer in the August heat. I was sweaty, grass covered, and almost finished. To welcome this visitor, I'd have to finish the job some other day and go get a shower and dress in clean clothes.

I was not a happy Quaker camper. I was job obsessed and not in the mood for chatting. *But,* I thought as I looked across the yard and saw Nancy weeding, *it's not all about me.* She tells me that all the time. So I put up the trimmer, took a shower, applied some cheerfulness along with my deodorant, and put on my freshly cleaned, grass-free glasses— ready to look for that of God in Nancy and my newish friend. And in everyone else I might encounter that day.

I say "that day" because this is something I seem to need to learn anew every day.

THAT OF GOD IN THEM? REALLY?

It's easy to accept the Quaker belief that the Bible tells us there is that of God in other people—at least as an idea. That's because when

I first think about it, I hear *There is that of God in* other people like me. So yeah, sure, there is that of God in other white male Quakers. I'll even concede white female Quakers. Quakers of all races. Even Quakers of all ages (though some of the YAFs—Young Adult Friends—are hard to take for an OAF—Old Adult Friend—like me). I even believe that about other Christians. Well, most other Christians.

Most of the time I can sorta get my head around how that might be translated in a vague, goodwill sense like the old, politically incorrect phrase "the brotherhood of man." After all, it was long said of Quakers that we believed in the fatherhood of God, the brotherhood of man, and the neighborhood of Germantown (Philadelphia, where many of us settled back in the day).

Actually, though, it's a radical, life-changing concept—if we really think about it. If, as George says, we're to answer that of God in everyone, that means *there is that of God in everyone.* Every one. Even him. Even her!

It means God treasures us equally (even if my friend Katie does wear a T-shirt that says "Jesus Loves Everybody...but I'm His Favorite"). We are all God's favorites. It's easy—on a good day—to see myself as one of God's favorites.

It means God treasures us equally. On a really good day I can see my family and friends as God's favorites. On my rare best days I can feel a sense that all 7+ billion of us on this planet are. Usually just a sense, though. I mean, seriously, God loves *everybody* as much as God loves me? If that's true, I'd better start treating people better. From my family to that panhandler outside the Reading Terminal.

Realizing that God loves us all equally is good for me. It begins to teach me humility. While I've often joked that I'm proud to be a humble Quaker, I struggle with ego. I need to heed the words of Paul, "Don't think of yourself more highly than you ought to think."

This concept, "that of God in everyone," was even more radical when Quakers first discovered it in Scripture. It was the seventeenth century, after all. This spiritual concept meant that the Friends began seeing people differently and treating them differently. For example, women. At the time Quakers came into being, there continued discussions about whether women even had souls. The Quakers affirmed that they did. And what's more they could preach and teach and travel in ministry away from their families every bit as much as any man could and better than some did.

Of course, as I said, it was the seventeenth century. Their views weren't universally embraced—except that a woman had as much right to be imprisoned or hung for her faith as any man. Just watch the Mary Dyer segment on Comedy Central's Drunk History if you don't believe me (danger: bad language there!).

And the equality was, to be honest, a different kind from what we know today. It was almost four hundred years ago, after all. Embracing this equality didn't immediately usher in universal suffrage or equal rights. But it was a start—and very radical for its time. Samuel Johnson expressed his opinion of a female Quaker preacher this way: "Sir, a woman's preaching is like a dog walking on his hind legs. It is not done well; but you are surprised to find it done at all."

Besides treating women more equally, they also took Galatians 3:28 to heart—"There is neither Jew nor Greek, there is neither slave nor free; nor is there male and female, for you are all one in Christ Jesus." And so they took trips around the world to call all sorts of people to the light of Christ that was already in them. They traveled throughout the Americas, the Caribbean, Europe, and more. In 1658 Mary Fisher felt led to visit the Ottoman Empire and share her faith with Sultan Mehmed IV. In 1658! Traveling on ship and then by foot, she reached the sultan's armed camp and asked for audience with him, saying she was an ambassador of "the Most High God." Ah, a truly humble Quaker. She was granted an audience, testified to the "universal light," and then, declining the sultan's offer of an armed escort (that whole Quaker peace thing again), she made her way alone back to Constantinople and eventually England.

That God loves everyone and sends the Divine Light to guide them is why Quakers have been in the forefront of such things as abolition of slavery, women's rights and suffrage, equal rights for all citizens, immigration reform, and much more. Not that we've gotten it right every time—we haven't always practiced the equality we preached. (For a number of good bad examples, see Fit for Freedom, Not for Friendship: Quakers, African Americans, and the Myth of Racial Justice by my friend Vanessa Julye and Donna McDaniel.) We still don't get it right. Many Quaker meetings are exceedingly white and middle class. But many of us are trying to live up to the ideal. And knowing what should be done and not always doing it are part of the humble stumble. Even Paul recognized that: "I don't know what I'm doing, because I don't do what I want to do. Instead, I do the thing that I hate.... The desire to do good is inside of me, but I can't do it. I don't do the good that I want to do, but I do the evil that I don't want to do."

One of the things to note about this passage—and it's true of the Quakers' failings in equality (and other areas!)—is that the failure is in the action, the carrying out of the conviction. The acting on the axiom. So we begin, despite failures, again and again to see all people have that of God in them: white, black, yellow, Christian, Hindu, Muslim, Buddhist, agnostic, atheist, rich man, poor man, beggar man, thief, deaf, sighted, blind, paraplegic, geniuses, those with Down syndrome, European, Asian, homeless woman, smart-mouthed teenager, bad driver, and so on.

But how do we live that out?

Quick Quaker Questions

Remember, no one right answer. What's your soul say?

- Am I open to and appreciative of everyone?
- Do I ever look at myself for evidence of prejudice—even that which may be buried?
- Do any of my beliefs or actions come from a bias about race, gender, sexual orientation, disability, class, and/or my own feelings of inferiority or superiority?
- Does my way of living show that the love of God includes affirming the equality of all people and treating others with consideration and esteem?

Stumbles in Bad Quaker History: Sit Anywhere You Like, Except...

While a good number of Friends were abolitionists or antislavery sympathizers, Quakers weren't necessarily welcoming to Blacks. Just as the Jim Crow South had colored-only restrooms, waiting rooms, dining rooms, and more, some Friends' meetings had benches that African-American attendees were required to sit on—under the stairs, in the back of the meetinghouse. Some meetings even had white "ushers" to prevent whites from sitting in the Black benches—and vice versa.

Begin at Home

"Don't look at me in that tone of voice." If I had a five-dollar bill for every time Nancy has said that to me, well, I'd have a lot of five-dollar bills. Looking at her in that tone of voice is one of my failings— it's a look that conveys irritation, exasperation, and frustration. A look nobody should get. Especially someone I love. Especially someone in whom I can easily (well, most of the time) see that of God.

So, before taking on seeing that of God in everyone in the entire world, it might be good for me to practice at home. After all, if I can't see it there, chances are I'm not going to be able to see it in some white supremacist or Islamic jihadist. Especially since I find both of those types really annoying and just plain wrong.

Well, maybe seeing God in a white supremacist or Islamic jihadist would be easier. After all, they are examples of people I will rarely run into. Or have to live with. Most of the time they are abstractions to me. Whereas my spouse, kids, neighbors, coworkers, and other regular contacts inhabit my life with all their imperfections. And drive me wacko at times.

Yes, imperfections. The idea of looking for that of God in everyone doesn't deny that the people in whom God dwells are imperfect. They're human, too! Just as I am. Imperfect. Just as I am.

The first step in my seeing that of God in everyone is seeing them as fully human as I see myself. And accepting them in that humanity. They are trying to live up to the leadings of God (even if they don't call it by that name) just as I am. Being a horrible human being is rarely on anybody's agenda. "I think I'll get up today and be a real jerk," said no one ever. They may have gotten up and acted like real jerks—but rarely, in their thinking, were they misbehaving. They had their reasons for doing the things they did. Fully justifiable (in their minds and hearts). Hmmm, just like me!

Part of the reason for looking for that of God in others is the whole love thing. It is really hard for me to be hateful to someone I love. Or should love. My good friend Connie taught me what she calls the SOB prayer. I use it a lot: "God, give that SOB everything I would hope for myself to be made happy, whole, and free."

"The caveat," Connie says, "is that you don't have to mean it but you have to say it at least once a day for at least two weeks, every time you think of the jerk! It'll change you."

And it does. Even if I don't want to be changed. No matter how good a mad I've got on.

As long as I look at someone through the eyes of "the mad," I can keep that hate heat banked and smoldering for quite a while. And I don't really look at them anyhoo; I look all around them. Above them, below them, beside them. But not into their eyes. When I look into their eyes, I begin to look into their souls, their eyes being the windows of their souls, as a sixteenth-century poet said. That's when I can see that of God there—loving them, guiding them. Even if they are jerks.

Another reason to look for God in them is so I can kindly call them to living up to it. In the same way I try to myself. As I pay attention to the promptings of God within my heart and soul, I begin to live more fully into the Spirit's presence. Sometimes it helps to have someone remind me to live in God's light. Such as when I'm at work and say something completely outrageous that is not quite true and my good friend Deborah cocks her head and gives me a look that says, *Really? Really??* Sigh, no, not really. I could be a little more careful with the truth.

I've learned two things that help me see that of God in others.

1. Make caring for others a daily practice. I come first. I am the center of my universe. Except, of course, I'm not. I need to balance my needs and wants with those of others—especially those others with whom I spend lots of time. As I care for people, they become less abstract and more real as children of God, worthy of the love, respect, and care I desire for myself. And by being kind, I model the deep, deep love of God.

2. Practice gratitude. Being thankful for the people who share life with me helps me see God's providing, watchful care over me. God has blessed me with these people in my life. All of them. I can whine about the

annoying ones (and shut down God's promptings of love in my own life) or I can be grateful for the gift of life and its varied experiences. Wow, that sounds like one of the "Deep Thoughts" by Jack Handey on *Saturday Night Live*, doesn't it? But it's true. Studies show that people who are in the habit of expressing gratitude are more likely to be helpful, generous, compassionate, and forgiving—and they're also more likely to be happy and healthy. (Wow, seeing that of God in others has health benefits? Who knew?)

QUICK QUAKER QUESTIONS

Remember, no one right answer. What's your soul say?

- Is my home a place of affection where God's presence is felt?
- Do I talk about God and life with my family and friends?
- Am I learning to be accountable for my own actions?

ALLIES

"Hispanics," muttered the cab driver as we drove west on Indianapolis's Washington Avenue. Nancy and I had just climbed off the train. It had arrived at 5:00 a.m., far too early to call family for a ride. It was the middle of a hotter-than-usual July. The air conditioning on the train had gone out. We were hot, tired, hungry, and ready for showers and some sleep. I, at least, was not ready for a racist screed.

But that's what I got as we made our way out through the city past buildings proclaiming *bodega, foto estudio, restaurante,* and more. "They're ruining our city," he moaned. "I wish they'd all just crawl back to Mexico."

Now I'd like to say that I rose up in righteous indignation and told him to shut up. Well, in a kinder but direct way. Or better yet, engaged him in a serious dialogue about bigotry and race in Indianapolis. But I didn't. I leaned my head against the window, shut my eyes, and tried to tune him out.

It wasn't one of my proudest moments.

It was a learning one, though. As I reflected on it later, I was reminded that seeing that of God in others was more than just an internal thing. Sometimes it requires action.

Sigh.

As an introvert, I'd just as soon keep things to myself. I truly believe that seeing that of God in others, and treating others as if they are equals, is something I need to put into practice. After all, if someone slighted Nancy, my kids, or my closest friends, I wouldn't hesitate to rush to their aid or defense. I wouldn't sit by quietly. How could I if I believed that the Hispanics in the neighbor-hood I had just passed through were equal to Nancy and me in our cab?

Double sigh.

How can I act as if I truly do believe there is that of God in every person?

Especially disconcerting, the more I thought about it, was that I remained silent that day while being in a position of power. I had lots of it! I had the power of being a customer. I had the power of a tip. I had the power to complain to his employer. And a fair amount of that power came from the position in society that I have as an educated, middle-class, white heterosexual male.

That privilege may not be something I aspire to or want. Society affords it to me regardless. While I believe, and try to live by the belief, that I am no better or more worthy than any of the other people in whom God's light shines, the fact is that some of those other people treat me differently. I notice this in a real way when I visit my bank in Philadelphia. One time I was wearing sunglasses and a hat (to keep my little bald head from getting sunburned). A sign there said, "Please remove any hats and sunglasses." I saw some Black men in front of me, holding their hats in their hands. I got in line with my hat firmly atop the great white expanse and my sunglasses still on. This was hard, as typically I am a rule keeper. But I wanted to see what might happen. The guard, who was Black, looked at me. But he didn't say anything. Some younger Black men came in and were promptly asked to take off their hats and sunglasses. I completed my transaction and was treated courteously. No one said a word about my hat or sunglasses.

I do this every time I visit that bank. Nobody's said anything to me yet. While men of color are regularly asked to doff their hats and glasses.

Which is why I'm finding it important, as a spiritual witness to my belief there is that of God in all people, to be an ally to those who are not treated equally because of their race, class, sexual orientation, ability, or gender. Being an ally is an action that puts me in touch with that of God in others in a tangible way. It helps me develop an understanding of the personal and institutional experiences different from mine, but equally imbued with God's light.

Part of that is pondering what I would experience now if I were a person of color, a woman, disabled, gay. Again, this is not a political exercise, but one I use as a child of God.

How can I act as if I truly do believe there is that of God in every person? Should I

- step into a situation in which a person of color is being ill-treated by someone who looks like I do? *Duh, yeah!*
- speak out about a situation in which I don't appear to have any vested interest? *Yepper.*
- interrupt a comment or joke that is insensitive or stereotypic

toward a target group, whether or not a member of that group is present? *Sure thing.*

- commit to the personal spiritual growth required to be genuinely supportive? *I guess so.*
- promote a sense of inclusiveness and justice in the places I work—and worship? *Getting a little touchy now.*
- create an environment that is hospitable for all—including at church? *You're kidding me, right?*
- share power inclusively? *You're really pushing it here, Jesus.*
- create opportunities for trust? *Gimme a break.*
- form authentic relationships with those who are "other"? *In my house? In my church? Show me that in the Bible! "Any immigrant who lives with you must be treated as if they were one of your citizens. You must love them as yourself." Oh. Never mind.*

If I'm going to be a friend of Jesus—which I endeavor to be!—I need to learn to be a vocal, public witness for His love of all people. This isn't easy for an introvert who likes to work quietly, even on Christian justice issues. Does this mean no more quiet taxi rides for this bad Quaker? If I get another bigoted taxi driver, do I have to engage him or her as a beloved child of God in a gentle but direct conversation about how I really don't want to be exposed to such thinking?

Yep. Either that or walk the ten miles home.

Sigh. Why isn't following the way of Jesus easier?

QUICK QUAKER QUESTIONS

Remember, no one right answer. What's your soul say?

- How do I speak up when I see someone treated poorly?
- In what ways do I respond to prejudice and injustice?
- What am I doing to help overcome the present effects of oppression?

Stumbles in Bad Quaker History: The Quaker Klanswoman

On the Muncie, Indiana, Friends Memorial Church pastors' wall of shame (that's what I call it—and my picture's there, too), hangs a picture of Daisy Douglass Barr. Barr was, in the early twentieth century, the pastor at Friends Memorial Church and a leader in the Women's Christian Temperance Union. She was also Imperial Empress of the Women's Ku Klux Klan with almost a quarter million members in Indiana and nearby states. She was so influential that, along with the Indiana Klan's Grand Wizard, D. C. Stevenson, she helped elect a Klan-friendly governor in Indiana in the mid-1920s!

ARE WE ALSO BLIND? UH, YEP!

I really dislike the story of Jesus healing the blind man in John 9. I mean, I'm happy for the blind man, but I'm a little uncomfortable with Jesus' dealing with the Pharisees. He's rough on 'em.

That story didn't use to bother me much. *Go gettum, Jesus,* I used to think. *Those self-righteous, privileged religious types deserve what You're putting to them.* Especially when He responds to one of their questions by saying, "If you were blind, you wouldn't have any sin, but now that you say 'We see,' your sin remains." *Yay, Jesus.* Of course, when I thought those thoughts I didn't think of myself as a self-righteous, privileged religious type. Over the years I've realized I probably am.

If I want my own faith-eyes opened, I have to first admit to my blindness.

I'm a Friendly Pharisee!

That's because now, when I read this passage, it lines like this:

Jesus said, "For judgment I have come into this world, so that the blind will see and those who see will become blind."

Brent and some other good Quakers who were with him heard him say this and asked, "What? Are we blind too?"

Jesus said, "Brent, my friend, if you were blind, you would not be guilty of sin; but now that you claim you can see, your guilt remains." (John 9:39-41 NBBV)

Ouch. Again. Why is He always picking on me?

I can easily imagine myself as one of the people Jesus was talking to on that Galilean street, robes wrapped tight around me, feeling a bit smug and more loved by God than some stinky blind beggar. As I move further into my wide-awake daydream, I see Jesus lecturing us, telling us how He had come so that those who were blind would be able to see, but that those who thought they could see would become blind. *Religious double-talk. Blind being able to see, the sighted becoming blind,* I would think. *What does it all mean? He is slick, all right. Ask Him a question and get questions instead of answers.*

Sometimes I've had enough. I want to walk away and just go back to my easier life, where I didn't worry about treating everybody else as a beloved child of God. I didn't worry about justice for all people. I didn't have to speak up in the face of evil. I...well...just didn't care so much, for Christ's sake. For Christ's sake, indeed! I can imagine His not saying anything else—just looking at me with the most amazingly penetrating eyes. Peering into my soul. Calling me wordlessly to love.

Am I blind to that of God in others? Sometimes, I'm 'fraid so. I'm blinded by my upbringing in a white-dominated society, my experiences (9/11, airplane bombings), and all sorts of other things. These things blind me so completely that I am unable to see in new ways—unless I decide to be healed by Jesus' touch.

The blind man knew he was blind.

The Pharisees did not.

If I want my own faith-eyes opened in order that I might see the fullness of life God wants me to have, I have to first admit to my blindness. I won't be able to see that of God in everyone until I begin the healing process.

As I do, as I'm touched by the ever-living, ever-loving Christ, I begin to see everything fresh and new. I need to ask with those people of old, "Are we also blind?" and drop the sarcasm from my voice.

Both are against my nature.

But they are the start to seeing with new eyes. Especially seeing that of God in everyone. Every one.

And acting on what I see.

CHAPTER 5

Truth Be Told

Integrity in an Often Duplicitous World

Integrity is a condition in which a person's response to a total situation can be trusted: the opposite of a condition in which he would be moved by opportunist or self-seeking impulses breaking up his unity as a whole being. This condition of trust is different from the recognition that he will always be kind or always tell the truth.

—*Kenneth C. Barnes*

The family is a place to practise [sic] being "valiant for the truth." We can live lives of integrity, letting both "yes" and "no" come out of the depth of truth within us, careful of the truth in all our dealings, so that our words and our lives speak the same message.

—*Elizabeth Watson*

Let your yes mean yes, and your no mean no. Anything more than this comes from the evil one.

—*Jesus*

Though I am not naturally honest, I am sometimes so by chance.
—*William Shakespeare*

"Oh, he's my pastor. He lies."

That's how Dorothea Bump introduced me. Dorothea was one of the women in the church I served who retired to Westminster Village in Muncie. Every month I had lunch with them in the dining room. I loved them all, but Dorothea was a favorite. She had been an award-winning reporter, a former city councilperson, and a list of other things too long to mention. And she had a wicked sense of humor.

That month Dorothea had drawn the short straw and was my hostess. We were making our way in to eat when one of the other residents chirped, "So who is the nice-looking young man you're with, Dorothea?" Without missing a beat, she shot her answer.

The look on her friend's face was worth the price of lunch.

Still, I did tease her a bit. "I don't lie. I make things up."

"Same thing," she quipped.

Well, the old-time Quakers would have agreed. Which is one reason I'm glad I'm a new-time Quaker. The old-time Quakers were known to be especially stringent about truth-telling—so no fiction, stage plays, or other entertainments were allowed. After all, such things are made-up. They aren't factually true.

A story is told about two Quaker boys who decided that it would be easy to trick a certain Friend who was "careful about the truth" (as we say) into telling a lie. One went to visit the old gentleman. Then, a while later, the second came along and knocked on the door. When the older Friend left the room to answer the knock, the first boy jumped out the window and ran toward home. When the door was opened, the second boy, expecting to catch the old man in a lie, asked if the first boy was there. The Friend carefully replied, "He was in the parlor when I left him."

There were actually lots of good reasons for being careful about the truth back then. And there are many reasons today.

I'm not lyin'!

ALL YOU NEED TO SAY IS SIMPLY YES OR NO

The main reason early Friends were careful about the truth was that Jesus told them to be. I guess I probably should listen to Jesus and live up to what He taught the way they did. The early Quakers called themselves "Friends" because Jesus said they were "if you do what I command you." That includes what He said in the Sermon on the Mount, which says:

> Again you have heard that it was said to those who lived long ago, *Don't make a false solemn pledge, but you should follow through on what you have pledged to the Lord.* But I say to you that you must not pledge at all. You must not pledge by heaven, because it's God's throne. You must not pledge by the earth, because it's God's footstool. You must not pledge by Jerusalem, because it's the city of the great king. And you must not pledge by your head, because you can't turn one hair white or black. Let your *yes* mean yes, and your *no* mean no. Anything more than this comes from the evil one.

That's why to this day Quakers don't take oaths or swear. Some of us may cuss, but we don't swear. Friends say yes and no and refuse to take oaths in court or elsewhere. Early Friends proved their truthfulness by their words and actions. In a day when merchants tried to gain advantage over others by overcharging and haggling, Quakers set what they considered fair prices for their goods and stuck to them. They would have been lousy used-car dealers.

They also made sure that what they sold was worthy of purchase. Terms of contracts were kept. Employees were treated in ways that matched what Quakers professed to believe. The Cadburys (yes of Crème Egg fame, yum!) moved their factory from a crowded city site to

English countryside to provide better air and surroundings for the people who worked for them. They also built a model village, Bournville, for their employees at the turn of the nineteenth century. Then they set up a trust to independently control the estate and provide things like schools, hospitals, and libraries. Today the village is home to around twenty-five thousand people.

That and other examples of Quaker integrity (those times when we got it right) all grow from our understanding that Jesus wasn't just talking about our words in the Sermon on the Mount. This Friendly culture of integrity in daily life gave Quakers a good reputation in the world. In business, it meant that by doing good, people like the Cadburys, the Lloyds (insurance), the Barclays (banking), and the Clarks (shoes) did well financially. Some of them very well, indeed.

It also meant that non-Friends began using the Quaker name on their products to signify good quality and honest value. That was okay when it was oatmeal. We weren't quite as happy with the Quaker Thermal Bath Cabinet of 1903. It was guaranteed to cure women's troubles, dropsy, catarrh, and more. It was endorsed by doctors, senators, and clerics—just no Quakers. The introduction of Quaker Cigars and Old Quaker Whiskey made us even less happy—though some Quakers have been known to smoke a cigar or have a dram of Scotch after a hard day of writing or tractoring. Not mentioning any names here, though.

This reputation for honesty is why, when I was called for jury duty a couple of years ago, the judge asked, "Does each of you swear or affirm that you will well and truly try the matter in issue between the parties, and give a true verdict according to the law and evidence?"

"Affirm." As a Quaker I affirm that I'll tell the truth because I'm telling the truth all the time. Well, at least I'm trying.

No matter what Dorothea Bump thought!

Quick Quaker Questions

Remember, no one right answer. What's your soul say?

- Am I careful to speak truth as I know it?
- Am I open to truth spoken to me, no matter where it comes from?
- Have I ever thought about governmental oaths implying a double standard of truth?

Stumbles in Bad Quaker History: I Spy a Bad Quaker

Whittaker Chambers was both a Quaker and a Communist spy. While he was part of a spy ring in the United States, he met Alger Hiss, who was also an active spy in the same cell. Hiss became an important figure in the U.S. State Department. Chamber outed Hiss as a Communist and a spy—much to Quaker congressman Richard M. Nixon's delight. Nixon then set out to prove Hiss a spy. Which history has confirmed he was.

You Can't Handle the Truth!

It's hard to always speak words that are true. Especially when our boss asks, "How's that project coming?" or our spouse inquires, "Does this make me look fat?" At least it is for me. I don't think I'm the only one. My friend and former golfing buddy Phil Ball had on his business card that in addition to being an MD, he was an MO—Master Obfuscator.

Maybe we can't handle the truth. Or at least telling it.

Sounds a lot better than *Liar*.

And sometimes speaking the truth is easier than living the truth. Even a liar like me finds it hard to twist the truth if I'm asked a question directly. But lying seems more prevalent in human nature. I mean, just look at one of the very first stories in the Bible. Those people are lyin' and blamin' all over the place—the serpent, Adam, Eve—well, everybody except God.

So maybe we can't handle the truth. Or at least telling it. We hear falsehoods all the time—from television ads ("It will remove every stain you've ever had and whiten your teeth, too"), from politicians ("I will lower taxes and raise the standard of living for everyone in my district"), and from home-repair contractors ("It'll be done in two weeks and under budget!"). There's an old joke that asks "How can you tell if an [insert your least favorite type of salesperson, merchant, politician here] is lying?" The answer is, "His (or her) lips are moving."

What's especially distressing is watching people lie while claiming they are telling the truth. One time, in a small town near where I lived, on a Tuesday a spokeswoman for a corporation told the press that rumors of layoffs and a plant closing at a local food canning company were a "non-story." The next morning at 10:30, 180 workers were informed that the plant was shutting down permanently. They were all out of work. Some non-story!

Examples like this are what make daily integrity so potent! We humans are so bad at telling the truth that we're stunned when someone (or some group) does. We recognize the truth and its power. We know that we are in the presence of someone who can be trusted. And we like it. Finally, the truth!

My friend Deborah is one such person for me. She is truly careful for the truth. If you ask her how she is, she will tell you. If you ask her how you are, she'll tell you! This is not some quirk of hers. It is part of her endeavor to live up to the Quaker way of integrity. To point others to a way of living that embraces integrity as a Christian witness and point people to Jesus.

Now the thing about Deborah's integrity is that she is not humorless or unkind. She laughs loudly at jokes that exaggerate or even at my obviously made-up stories. And she does not use her honesty to inflict pain on anybody. She is not *honest to a fault* or *brutally honest* in the sense that such honesty often wounds. She is not *diplomatically honest*—couching the truth in all sorts of qualifiers to soften the blow—either. She speaks the truth but is care-full with her words and how she says them. She models straightforward integrity coupled with lovingkindness.

Which is a good way to think about the practice of honesty for ourselves. How can I speak with integrity and kindness?

QUICK QUAKER QUESTIONS

Remember, no one right answer. What's your soul say?

- What do I do to maintain the integrity of my inner and outer lives?
- Do I act on my principles even when this entails difficult consequences?
- Am I honest and truthful in all that I say and do, even when compromise might be easier or more popular?

HOW MUCH TRUTH DO I HAVE TO TELL?

I am not the sort of fellow who goes in for special ringtones for individual callers. Well, I used to have the Hallelujah Chorus play when family called. But I ditched that phone long ago. Nowadays I assign most people my standard ringtone, which is the theme song from Mr. Deity, a satirical online show where God is a movie producer.

One day, in the midst of meetings and preparation for a trip to Washington, DC, I missed a call. When I got back to my desk I discovered a message from my friend and onetime (so far) coauthor, Beth.

"Hi. I know you'll be flying tomorrow. I hope you survive the flight," sang her bright, cheery voice.

Hope you survive the flight? Yikes!

Except I knew what she meant. Beth knows I hate (as in scared to death and in dire need of tranquilization) flying. So what I heard was her concern for me.

Still, it was a bit disconcerting—"I hope you survive the flight."

Then she tried to cover up by explaining what she meant... and, of course, just dug a deeper hole. I was really laughing by the time I called her back.

But it did make me wonder: how many times have I said something that sounded so right in my mind but came out so wrong aurally? Especially to the listener? How many times have I tried to say something helpful and said something hurtful? Far too many, I am afraid.

It also made me think of the grace we extend to those we love. If an "enemy" of mine had said those words, I would have resented them. I would have heard those words as a dig at my frequent failure of nerve. But since they came from Beth, a good friend, I heard them as care and compassion about something she knows troubles me. Even if she does not have that fear herself.

I also remembered the old gospel hymn "Open My Eyes," especially the second verse: *"Open my ears, that I may hear voices of truth thou sendest clear, / And while the wave-notes fall on my ear, everything false will disappear."*

Indeed, the false disappeared in the truth of Beth's call. The truth was that she reached out in Christian love and offered a wish for my fear to be eased and my travels to be smooth. Ah, let's hear it for intentions of grace and love.

I think the secret to living with integrity centers on lives of intention and love. Intention and love mean that I am care-full of the words I use and the actions I take. Not just what I say, but how I say it. Not just what I do, but how I do it. (Oops. I guess that means I have to learn to speak, and live, the truth in love.)

Of course, in any discussion of truth, some smart aleck always brings up the question of degrees of truth implicit in ethical dilemmas. If you were hiding Jews during World War II and the Nazis came to your house and asked where they were, would you tell them, thereby being honest but causing innocent death?

Really?

How often—for most of us—is this sort of situation going to arise? I'm more likely to be asked, "Do you know how fast you were going?" by a state highway patrolman.

To which I'm likely to respond, "Yes, I do. Do you?"

I think the Nazi question begs the issue. It turns the problem from one of integrity to one of how *dishonest* I am allowed to be. What's the limit? How far can I go? How truthful must I be? If I can lie acceptably in this instance, what other times can I sacrifice the truth? When the officer who pulls me over asks if I know how fast I was going, can I say no just because I haven't looked at the speedometer during the last few minutes—even though I was sailing by every other car on the highway?

It's like the time I was a college freshman and I answered the one telephone on our dorm floor in Penn Hall. I picked it up and said, as I usually did, "Penn Hall. Who in the hall do you want?"

There was a gasp from the other end of the line. Finally, the person sputtered, "Such impertinence. Do you know who this is?" I allowed that I did not and the woman said, "This is Mrs. X [the college president's wife]!"

I replied meekly, "Do you know who this is?"

"No," she said, waiting for me to reveal myself.

"Good," I said and hung up.

Truth-telling is tricky. I certainly didn't want her to know my name—especially after I found out hers. And sometimes Quakers have minced, diced, and sliced the truth. Levi Coffin, a nineteenth-century Friend who worked on the Underground Railroad, was summoned into court when some slave hunters convinced a local man to have Friend Levi charged with harboring fugitive slaves. Which he was doing. His neighbors from tiny Newport (now Fountain City), Indiana, were summoned as witnesses. He writes that he wasn't worried about being convicted because if he was, he would serve as a witness to the horrors of slavery and how God-loving people should stand against it.

So far, so good. As in behaving truthfully.

When Coffin took the stand, the person bringing the charges asked if he understood the Fugitive Slave Law.

> I told him that I had read it, but did not know whether I understood it or not. I suggested that he turn to it and read it, which he did. I told him that I knew of no violation of that statute in our neighborhood. Persons often traveled our way and stopped at our house who said they were slaves, but I knew nothing about it from their statements, for our law did not presume that such people could tell the truth.

Coffin reports that this caused a laugh throughout the court-room—except from his questioner. He went on to say:

> A company of seventeen fugitives had stopped at my house, hungry and destitute, two of them suffering from wounds inflicted by pursuers who claimed them as slaves, but I had no legal evidence that they were slaves; nothing but their own statements, and the law of our State did not admit colored evidence. I had read in the Bible when I was a boy that it was right to feed the hungry and clothe the naked, and to minister to those who had fallen among thieves and were wounded, but that no distinction in regard to color was mentioned in the good Book, so in accordance with its teachings I had received these fugitives and cared for them.

Coffin did not prevaricate. Or waver. He spoke the truth. But he spoke it at a slant by using his persecutors' words against them and bringing in truth from the Bible. Was he truthful? Did he speak with integrity? Was he a good Friend—or does he warrant his own Stumble in Bad Quaker History? I'll leave that for you to decide. As I will what that story says to you about truthfulness in your life.

Though Coffin was not convicted for or by his words, other Friends have been—including the afore-mentioned Mary Dyer. Dyer was a Quaker who ended up being hanged simply because she was a Quaker—which the late seventeenth-century Bostonians had banned from Massachusetts. As a result of the integrity of her life and faith commitment, she kept returning to proclaim her understanding of the gospel. So they hanged her.

Remember the power true words and actions have!

Whether we're confronted by traffic cops, Nazis, bosses, spouses, or whoever, Jesus commands us to speak and live the truth.

That is easier if we remember the power true words and actions have!

Despite the potential cost.

QUICK QUAKER QUESTIONS

Remember, no one right answer. What's your soul say?

- Am I honest and truthful in all I say and do?
- Do I maintain strict integrity in business transactions and my dealings with others?
- Do I use money and information entrusted to me with discretion and responsibility?

BUT TRULY, HOW CAN I BE HONEST ALL THE TIME?

Living with complete integrity is a pretty tall order. Especially when we know that telling the truth, the whole truth, and nothing but the truth could get us in a world of hurt with our significant others, let alone the authorities.

In his book *For Everything a Season*, Phil Gulley urges his readers that if they're ever going to buy a used car, they should "buy one from a Quaker. If you ask, we'll tell you everything that's wrong with the car and whether it's been wrecked. But you have to ask, because we won't volunteer the information. We're honest, but not stupid."

Well, of course, he's speaking tongue firmly in cheek. But the point is clear—we are to be honest, even if it sometimes means being judged stupid by the world's standards.

So a life of intention and integrity should be one of our goals today. I mean, think about it. Can I live so much in the power of the Spirit that my life would be one of transparent truth? Besides shocking the others, I would be a beacon of integrity in a world filled with the darkness of lies. So would you! In 1925, the London Yearly Meeting of the Religious Society of Friends, the official association of Quakers in Britain, said,

> If we would indeed take a place in God's larger work, more is required of us than the ordinary virtues of respectability. The law of "thou shalt not" is superseded by Christ's command "be ye perfect." The basis of Christianity is laid deeper than in the maintenance of a certain moral minimum. Yet it would be foolish to ignore the difficulties which beset us, as from day to day we face afresh the task of living cleanly. To none is a life of sincerity, integrity, purity and industry easy. But for the grace of God, it is impossible.... But personal loyalty to Christ will always be the strongest anchorage in treacherous waters. It is through this allegiance that power for life is received.

If I am a natural-born liar (if what Dottie Bump said is true), I have to make continual checks. I have to get in a space where there's a spiritual subliminal loop running through my soul, constantly questioning:

- Are my words and actions right now flowing out of what I believe?

- Are they coming from love as the first impulse—or ego, anger, or the need to be right?
- Will these actions and words reflect to others what I say I believe or some incomplete gospel?
- Are these words and actions really true *and* necessary?
- Can I listen to another's truth with grace and acceptance?

Hmmm...maybe it's just easier to skip telling the truth.

Except I want to be known as a man of integrity. Living truthfully is a form of witness to the action of the Spirit in my life—continually changing me into the person God and I both want me to be. It's one thing to be known, humorously, as a bad Quaker. It's quite another to have people really believe I am because of the way I've acted or spoken. And my speaking, in an almost instantaneous way, shows the soil in which my words were grown.

I am slowly learning ways of living with integrity. Sometimes I need to suck it up and take responsibility for my actions and their results. I lack confidence at the best of times, so to admit that I messed up feeds my inner insecurities. For that reason, I'm a sorta un-hip Fonzie from *Happy Days*—I have a hard time saying the word *sorry*. I

Can I, as a friend of Jesus, be trusted?

mean, I may not intend to hurt you, but my lack of integrity or hurtful words may wound you all the same. Can I, as a Jesus follower, own that? Can I say, "I was wrong" instead of "I was wrong [but I was in a bad mood, something you did really pissed me off, I didn't mean to hurt you]"? I'm still learning how cultivating integrity means accepting responsibility for my words and actions—intentional or not.

Likewise, can I keep my commitments? If I say I'll do something, do I follow through? In a timely way? I haven't always. I've always meant to. When I was a teenager and I bought my friend Greg's Wollensak

5280 reel-to-reel tape recorder (we were budding audiophiles back then), I promised to pay him ten dollars a month until it was paid off. It would take five months. I made the first two payments. Then... well, he was in Colorado and I was in Ohio and I had a girlfriend I liked to take to the movies and something else would come along that I wanted to buy and he got really mad and it hurt our friendship.

He didn't want to confront me.

I didn't like being confronted.

Can I, as a friend of Jesus, be trusted? If not... hmmm, what does that say about how good a friend I am of His?

QUICK QUAKER QUESTIONS

Remember, no one right answer. What's your soul say?

- Do I take care of items entrusted to me?
- Am I avoiding spending beyond my means via the use of credit cards?
- Do I tell the truth that needs to be told?

TRUTHINESS

In 2005, on the pilot of *The Colbert Report*, Stephen Colbert coined a term that many Americans chuckle over—"truthiness." According to him, "Truthiness is 'What I say is right, and [nothing] anyone else says could possibly be true.' It's not only that I *feel* it to be true, but that *I* feel it to be true. There's not only an emotional quality, but there's a selfish quality."

Christian integrity is not "truthiness." It is not about what we feel to be true or about us. It is about, as early Quakers call it, "that which is eternal," by which they meant those spiritual truths that are deeper than reason or intellect and existed "before the world was." It's what we, even those of us who are bad, are called to live up to and into. That which is eternal is the love, grace, and integrity of God. It is that we are called into newness of creation and life. It is that we are meant to be "true" as a door that hangs correctly is—true to its purpose and function. And even as out of kilter as humanity is, it can be brought back, through the power of the Spirit, to true. To plumb. As George B. Jeffery said:

> Jesus saw the truth that men needed and he thought it urgent that that truth should be proclaimed. That trust is handed on to us, but it is a responsibility from which we shrink. We feel that we have a very imperfect grasp of the meaning of the Gospel. Perhaps, after all the earnest seeking of the Church, we are only beginning to see the tremendous implications of it. We dimly see that this Gospel, before it has finished with us, will turn our lives upside down and inside out.

I would be true. Would you?

CHAPTER 6
GOD'S GOOD GREEN EARTH

The Call to Care for Creation

The produce of the earth is a gift from our gracious creator to the inhabitants, and to impoverish the earth now to support outward greatness appears to be an injury to the succeeding age.
—John Woolman

As a Religious Society of Friends we see the stewardship of God's creation as a major concern. The environmental crisis is at root a spiritual and religious crisis; we are called to look again at the real purpose of being on this earth, which is to till it and keep it so as to reveal the glory of God for generations to come. It is a stony road ahead but our faith will uphold us; the power to act is God's power which is mediated through each of us as we give and receive support one from another. We can all listen if we will to the sounds of the earth, tuning into it with joy.
—London Yearly Meeting

You will love your neighbor as yourself.
—Jesus

There will be a rain dance Friday night, weather permitting.
—George Carlin

Why am I mowing the side of a hill? That was the second thought I had while out on a verdant hillside on a beautiful, azure-skied late-spring day. That thought came to me because I was viewing the grass and sky from a perspective that was all wrong. The tractor I was mowing with had just tipped over and was starting to roll sideways down the hill.

My first thought was *I'm gonna die.*

That's because about 130 people a year do when they roll a tractor. I figured I was going to be number 131. My body sorta took over: my left foot pushed in the clutch to disengage the transmission, my left hand reached down to shut off the power take-off to the mower (my ears could hear the big blades going whomp, whomp, whomp behind my head), my right foot went out to prop the tractor up and keep it from rolling (as if a little leg with weak ankles is going to stop a one-ton tractor, lift bucket, and mower from tipping), my right foot pulled back in as the weight of the tractor began to settle uncomfortably on my ankle, my right hand checked that the seat belt was tight, my eyes closed . . . and gravity took over. On its side the tractor went, sliding a few feet down the hill's sandy soil. I went along for the ride. It took forever.

It was a long one. Not for my neighbor David Jay, who, at that very moment, was coming across the bridge down the road from me and saw it happen. But an eternity for me. I have never been a math or science whiz, but I saw the truth in Einstein's theory of relativity. Time slowed waaay down. Slooowww motion down.

I didn't die.

The Rollover Protection System (ROPS) installed on all tractors built after 1985 did what it was supposed to do. My only casualties were a sore ankle and a massively bruised ego.

David pulled up about the time I started breathing again. "Roll a tractor?" he asked drolly.

"No, thanks," I replied, "just rolled one."

My smartaleckness really comes out when I'm scared.

David and one of his farmhands got the tractor upright. I was too shaky to do anything but watch. He also promised not to tell my wife (whose last words to me as I left the house that morning were "Be careful on the hill. It's very easy to roll a tractor"). I put the tractor away. Walked in the house. Nancy asked, "Why are you so white?"

"Rolled the tractor," I said, took a shower, and slept for three hours.

As I drifted off, I thought, *Why was I mowing the side of a hill?*

It's a good question. How I've become a conservation-minded fellow is beyond me. It must be evidence of God's slow but steady work in my soul—sorta like the slow, steady work of the Colorado River on what is now known as the Grand Canyon. I only hope that someday my soul is as beautiful as that natural masterpiece.

It's not that I've ignored the earth in my long short-legged life. Indeed, I was a Cub Scout, a Boy Scout, an Indian Guide, and Christian Service Brigade member. As kids, my cousins and buddies and I often camped out in the summer, albeit many times in our city backyards. My granddad, dad, and his friends went camping and fishing and dragged me along at times, often to the Hocking Hills in southern Ohio. I had appreciation for natural beauty but was a bit disconnected from it. I lived in a city in an era before urban hiking/biking trails, and intentional green spaces meant part of the blacktopped playground was painted with industrial green paint. It was also a time that we thought our biggest dangers were God-less Russians and their H-bombs and not our own overextension of natural resources and pollution of air and water.

Doh!

I started waking up to the need for care of the earth as a freshman in college (I began waking up to a lot of things that year!). On April 22, 1970, just a few weeks before the Kent State massacre, the first Earth Day was held. It seemed like a good thing. Who could be against taking care of our planet? Even our Evangelical Quaker college observed it (not by letting us out of class, however). Plus it was sorta fun to dress up and have a mock funeral for the earth. My college buddy Bill Roman donned a cassock and carried a book of prayer while a group of other students served as pallbearers and grave diggers.

But conservation seemed a hippie-ish, radical sort of thing. Never mind that I had grown up attending John Burroughs Elementary School, named for one of the most famous naturalists and conservationists of his day. And the man who said, "I still find each day too short for all the thoughts I want to think, all the walks I want to take, all the books I want to read, and all the friends I want to see." Which well reflects how I feel.

Still, for years, despite witnessing a longtime involvement in caring for the earth by many of my friends who are Friends, doing so myself was not much on my radar. I mean, I tried to do no real harm—which was pretty easy since I didn't own any smoke-belching, pollution-producing factories. Nor did I worry about my oil platforms in the Gulf of Mexico and elsewhere leaking and spilling thousands of gallons of crude into the ocean. I had no oil platforms. I didn't strip-mine. I didn't mine at all. I didn't use massive amounts of fertilizer to increase crop production. The only crop I had was usually the grass growing on the city lot around my house.

And now I find myself living in an Energy Star–rated house that's extremely efficient and heated and cooled by a geothermal system. And that's just the outward manifestation of the gradual inward change.

What happened?

Faith happened. The slow arc of God's grace and teaching has brought home to me this idea that it's not enough just for me to bemoan (and smirk a bit about) the Cuyahoga River being so polluted that it caught fire the summer between my high school and college years (an event memorialized by Randy Newman's "Burn On"). Nope, I actually have to do something.

If, that is, I believe in God and want to be a Friend of Jesus.

QUICK QUAKER QUESTIONS

Remember, no one right answer. What's your soul say?

- What are the spiritual implications of the way I treat the earth/ nature?

PRIUSES OR PRIUII?

Every summer almost 1,500 Quakers converge on a college campus somewhere in North America for a week known as Gathering. In 2014, it was at California University of Pennsylvania.

Um, shouldn't California University be in California? Confusing, eh? What made it even more confusing was that California, Pennsylvania, where the university is located is not a major metro area. It's a town of about 6,800 folks nestled in a bend on the Monongahela River. People were a mite worried about finding the place. On Facebook, one wag wrote, "Just look for the line of Priuses with peace and earth care bumper stickers and follow them."

Good advice. Sure enough, when I got there and I looked around at the cars coming in, the percentage of hybrid cars was huge. Quakers do probably buy more Priuses (or is that Priuii—I've never been able to figure out the plural for Prius?) percentagewise than any other faith group. It's not because they're trendy (the car

We think our world is God's creation in the same way that each one of us is.

101

or the Quakers) but because of this whole care-for-the-earth thing. We love God so we also love God's good earth. We think our world is God's creation in the same way that each one of us is. So we try to heed the call to be good stewards of this planet during our lifetimes and for those who come after us, remembering, as John Woolman said, that "to impoverish the earth now to support outward greatness appears to be an injury to the succeeding age." That's why so many Friends were among the four hundred thousand folks who participated in the People's Climate March in New York City in 2014. It's not just because they're good people or it's a good political stand. It's because their faith led them to do it.

I often joke that, as a Quaker, I'm not a member of an organized religion. If you ever come visit us and stick around awhile, you'll see what I mean. We're always waiting to see what God is telling us to do. We often have various takes on what God's direction is so we have to sift through them all to discern what God is really telling us to do and not what we think God wants us to do because it matches exactly what we as humans think ought to be done.

Confusing, eh? Then we'll appoint a committee with a subcommittee with a working group to discern if the discernment was right on. Then it'll come back up the Quaker ladder for further discernment. And then...maybe...just maybe...some action.

That process can take a long time (it took Quakers as a group almost a century to decide that slavery was not a good thing!). One thing that many of us have agreed on, though, is that caring for the earth is a spiritual enterprise. At a personal level, that's one reason you see so many hybrid or high-mpg vehicles (and so few Hummers) parked in front of a Quaker meetinghouse. Likewise, while the percentage of the farmers among us has tumbled in the last century, those who remain often practice responsible farming practices.

My friend Katrina, for example, runs the family farm her parents founded in the 1970s. Meeting Place Organic Farm sits in southwest Ontario, Canada. Katrina's family farms organically with Belgian horses and has a mixed livestock operation designed to nourish the soil and produce food in an ecologically sustainable manner. While that may sound vaguely Amish, trust me, I've never seen bubbly Katrina dressed anywhere close to a staid young Amish woman. If she's wearing black, it's a fashionable little black dress and she's stepping out for a night on the town. And step out on the town Katrina does.

In my own case, the land we steward has all been taken out of agricultural production and converted to tallgrass prairie or forest. This is a big change for me—a man who once saw this land as a potential development and a possible source of monetary wealth. All because of faith and an increasing awareness of the fragility of our ecosystem and the vanishing species here in the Midwest. It is rather affirming to see butterflies, for example, in places where there weren't any fewer than ten years ago.

Besides individual efforts, we Friends actually have some groups that work directly on the issue. Quaker Earthcare Witness takes Spirit-led action to address the ecological and social crises of the world from a spiritual perspective, emphasizing Quaker process and testimonies. My friend Katherine, a writer like me, is their publications person. She works with QEW because, as she says,

> Ever since I was a little girl, I've met God in nature—in the light, in the sky, in trees, flowers, and animals. I've had a reverence for all life because God loved it, and even as a child I would make it my job to clean up streams (and even a drainage ditch by my house) because I knew caring for creation was caring for God.

I have a number of other Friend-friends who work with the Earth Quaker Action Team. Its goal is to build a just and sustainable economy through nonviolent direct action. They led a strategic effort to get

PNC Bank out of the business of financing mountaintop removal coal mining. They used nonviolent direct action to shine the light on PNC Bank's role as one of the primary financiers of this devastating surface mining practice.

My friend (and Friend) Eileen Flanagan, an amazing writer and spiritual teacher, is the clerk and active in this group.

> I'd been growing increasingly concerned about climate change when, in February 2011, I had a strong intuition to attend the Philadelphia Flower Show. Although none of the friends I'd invited were available, I kept feeling that I needed to go on a particular day, which turned out to be exactly when EQAT was protesting PNC Bank's financing of companies engaged in mountaintop removal coal mining. PNC was also a major sponsor of the Flower Show, so here were all these Friends—several of whom I knew—singing and handing out fliers in front of the PNC pavilion. There was something about their mixture of joy and courage that really touched me, so I grabbed a stack of flyers and joined them. I felt that God had given me the nudge I needed.

Katrina, Katherine, and Eileen are not bad Quakers like I am, but they're certainly bad in other (better) ways. And, again, all of this comes from a spiritual—not a do-gooder—base.

These folks aren't a bunch of whacked-out, aging hippie types either. If you saw them on the street, you'd think they were as normal as you are. And they pretty much are. Except for Katrina. And she's normal in her own unique way. What they have in common is that they've heard the voice of the Spirit calling them to action in caring for the earth—and often that call is tied in with their views on peace, simplicity, equality, and more.

What canst thou say about caring for the earth as a spiritual practice? More importantly, what canst thou do?

Even more importantly, what canst I do?

Quick Quaker Questions

Remember, no one right answer. What's your soul say?

- How might I transform my life as witness to a right spiritual relationship with the earth and God in active stewardship?

Stumbles in Bad Quaker History: A Whale of Time

Quakers dominated the New England whaling industry for almost 150 years. These good, peaceable people with their tolerant labor practices, honest business dealings, and views of equality (many blacks, including escaped slaves, found work on the whale ships) waged wholesale war on whales. Thousands of whales were slaughtered to satisfy the need for lamp oil, buggy whips, ivory for piano keys, tops of walking sticks, carriage springs, corset stays, fishing rods, frames for women's hats, skirt hoops, toys, and other necessities. Oh, and they got very rich doing it, too!

Divine Inaction, Godly Action, or Spiritual LOAFing

"Brent is a gentleman farmer. He lives on fifty acres being reclaimed into prairie and woodlands. That mean he raises grass and trees. Now, as I understand it, grass grows on its own. And trees do, too. So he gets to sit and watch them and read books and think deep thoughts. My thought is: that's the kind of farmer I want to be!"

That's how I was introduced prior to giving a speech one time. Everybody chuckled, of course, including me. It was a witty introduction. But part of it nagged at me a bit and I still (obviously) remember it from time to time. Especially on those days I'm out working in those trees and grass.

Yes, the thousands of trees that have been planted over the years will grow on their own—as long as they're kept free of weed entanglement and damage from deer who like to munch on tender young shoots or rub the bark of growing trees. That means weeding, mowing, and tying strips of dryer fabric softener sheets on each one. (The deer hate the scent as much as I do. Let me tell you, that's a lot of cutting and tying. And the prairie has to be burned to kill off the woody growth and destroy weeds. Some, though, don't seem to mind the fire. So we have to deal with the bazillion thistle rosettes (that's a baby thistle, I've learned) that sprout after the fire.

That, in part, is what I'm called to do. But before I was called to that work, I had to be convinced it was important spiritual work. Otherwise, I was just being another do-gooder. There's nothing wrong with that, but I'm not a natural do-gooder. So for me to be one, God sorta has to kick my rear end and say, "Pay attention, Brent. You need to do this."

My first conscious efforts toward earth care as intentional Spirit work began small: little things like getting rid of incandescent lightbulbs, wrapping the water heater in a cover, buying a high-mpg car, buying energy-efficient appliances when the old ones needed replacing. Tiny steps for a tiny soul.

As my soul grew, and an opportunity came to build a house, we designed it to be energy-efficient from its six-inch-thick insulated sidewalls, eight-inch-thick insulated roof, triple-insulated windows, geothermal heating and cooling system, and more. Now this wasn't cheap. Which kept grating on my desire to live simply. Doesn't *simple* mean *cheap*?

The question came down to What is *this* bad Quaker to do?

It wasn't that I couldn't afford it. I could. The fact that I could afford it…and more, all rubbed up against my perceptions of what it meant for a person of faith to care for the earth and live simply. A hut? Give all my money away? Give the land away? Get a horse and buggy?

Which is the thing about the Quaker way. Jesus' way. It's not so easy sometimes. The values it gives us sometimes fit easily together.

Other times, not so much.

What's a bad Quaker to do?

After lots of wrestling, the question came down to *What is* this *bad Quaker to do?* There's no universal answer to what it means to live simply or to care for the earth. Which is part of the delight and frustration of being Friends of Jesus. We are called to determine, with Divine assistance, what is ours to do in this world. About peace. Justice. Truth. Simplicity. Care for the earth.

Phooey! Please, God, can't You just type out instructions and send them to me?

But joy comes from discovering and working with God in the redemption of this world and our souls. As I've done this, I've found myself led into new places of growth as I listened to God and discerned how I could be a more responsible consumer, what wasteful household habits I had, and how to use my resources more responsibly.

My life is full of possibilities. I can join a community-supported agriculture effort. Help at our meeting's (church's) community garden. Am I called to work for national legislation that regulates or prohibits the use of genetically engineered food? Or maybe I should just LOAF —buy food that is Local, Organic, Animal-Friendly, and Fairly produced and traded.

Of course, the issue is not that there are endless ways that I could be involved. There are plenty of things I *could* do. The issue is what is God calling me *to* do.

The same is true for you. It's not helpful to be guilted into doing something by other people (even this bad Quaker). Such action may be "good," but it doesn't feed your soul. Ask what feels right for your life.

What fits—not what is forced. If it doesn't feel right to you to create a wildlife sanctuary in your backyard and/or on church property, then don't. Not until you feel it is right and fit and from God. If a leading to make your own naturally based cleaning products; to compost all organic waste—and recycling paper, cardboard, cans, and bottles; to reduce the greenhouse gas emissions associated with landfills; to sell your car and rely solely on a bike or public transit, and so on is truly from God, it will persist. It won't let you go and will work on your soul. It will also

- come with a sense of joy.
- feel life giving, not life draining.
- give you the power and will to actually do it!

QUICK QUAKER QUESTIONS

Remember, no one right answer. What's your soul say?

- Am I engaged in positive ways of nurturing and deepening my relationship with creation?

DOING UNTO OTHERS

For me the easiest thing about caring for the earth is the *how*. The *why* is harder. At least it's more complex. While I can search the scriptures for words about why I should care for the earth, some of them seem a bit of a stretch. I mean, to read about Jesus' ruling the wind and the waves doesn't really tell me that I need to! Or even can. I've prayed for clear weather on days of big softball games, golf matches, or family gatherings, and the rain poured down! While "The effectual fervent prayer of a righteous man availeth much," I've found that the fervent prayer of a bad Quaker availeth rain and other bad weather.

It is true that Scripture says, "The earth is the LORD's and everything in it, the world and its inhabitants too." But since it's the Lord's, why do I need to care for it? When I lived in Muncie, Indiana, the public works department didn't think humanity was responsible for the earth. Munsonians often joked that since God put the snow on our streets, the DPW waited for God to remove it.

Besides, people use other Bible verses (especially in the King James version) to justify using up all the resources: "And God blessed them, and God said unto them, Be fruitful, and multiply, and replenish the earth, and subdue it: and have dominion over the fish of the sea, and over the fowl of the air, and over every living thing that moveth upon the earth."

Of course, "You must keep my decrees and my laws....And if you defile the land, it will vomit you out as it vomited out the nations that were before you" seems a pretty clear (and graphic) justification for taking care of this planet.

For me, in all my badness, there is an even greater reason: it's the connection between earth care, peace, looking for that of God in others rooted in Jesus' own life and example. Much of Jesus' work consisted of caring for the poor and oppressed in the society of His day. He fed, healed, and cared for the less fortunate—and confronted the privileged with their resources for not doing so. He more than hinted that we, as His followers, were to participate in the kin-dom of God—the interrelationship of all creation that brings universal *shalom*.

Taking care of the earth is part of that participation.

How? Well, that may not be apparent on the surface. But when you stop to think that we in the so-called developed countries on this planet use and misuse resources, it's obvious we have to be causing real harm to those unfortunate enough to be born in those less-developed places. Remember when I talked about the seeds of war in our possession, especially as they relate to the Congo? One report says that 30 percent of kids in the Congo drop out of school so they can go work in the mines. The minerals mined are used mostly to produce goods consumed in the Western world. In the United States. In Indiana. In my home. My "need" for coltan dragged from the earth by extreme methods means their lack of education.

That's in addition to the huge disparity of my resource use compared to that of a person in India. The United States, for example, has only 5 percent of the world population but uses 20 percent of the world's energy.

I'm pretty certain that all this disparity in using the earth's resources is not what Jesus has in mind for me if I'm to be part of ushering in the kingdom of God.

This is not about blame. Or guilt. It is about being aware of how our actions impact those children of God we will never see—and rarely think about. It's about our being Friends of Jesus in a way that is possible now that wasn't when He walked the shores of Galilee.

Think of it. I now know that what we do impacts others around the world in a way that generations before could not. A smart bomb dropped in Syria while I'm watching *House Hunters* on HGTV is witnessed shortly after it happens—though I rarely count the innocent dead who are "collateral" damage. And I rarely count the resource costs, natural and economic, that it took to make that bomb "smart," fly it around the world, and drop it on the people below.

Well, actually I do. Despite all my badness, this waste really bothers me because the resources used for one bomb (let alone thousands of them) takes food from the mouths of poor children. Think what forty thousand dollars (the average cost of such a bomb) could mean for feeding the hungry children in our own neighborhoods. Of which there are sixteen million in the United States.

And while it's easy to decry government spending on such things, what about my own need to have inexpensive clothes, food, and cars? "If you want to be perfect, Brent, go, sell your possessions and give to the poor" (Matthew 19:21 NBBV). Whoa! I don't need to be perfect, Jesus...just pretty good. What do I have to do for that? "Sorry, Brent, be perfect, therefore, as your heavenly Father is perfect" (Matthew 5:48 NBBV).

Well, ouch, Jesus. You really didn't have to go there. No "out," eh?

How am I supposed to care for the poor and oppressed and the earth while simultaneously taking their labor and natural resources? I hate it when Jesus gets all preachy on me. Especially when it's something I need to be preached at about.

QUICK QUAKER QUESTIONS

Remember, no one right answer. What's your soul say?

- Do I strive to practice active ways of living in harmony with the earth and all the people on it?

We were thrown out of a garden. Not just my badself, but all of us. At least that's what Genesis 3 tells us. It's a sad story, mostly, of wily, talking snakes, gullible people who refuse to accept responsibility: "The woman made me...." "The serpent made me...." Sin reared its ugly head and separated woman and man from the ideal in which God had placed them. Adam and Eve were driven from the garden, ripped from idyllism to realism, the reality being that death had come into the world. And what had they done? Surrounded by abundance, they had to have one thing more—one thing they didn't need and were warned to stay away from.

That's never happened to me. Well...it doesn't happen every day. Well...every hour, anyhow.

Still, I am struck by the sadness of the exile. I think of the life of ease in Eden, in total communion with God's good creation, and God and I mourn. And I wonder how the exile has impacted creation—not just humankind. Since that time of abundance and love, with God, humanity, and creation in complete harmony, we have acted as little gods and begun using up the earth for our benefit.

We build larger and larger cities. We dig more and more minerals from the earth. We do things that kill off greater and greater numbers of species. We buy newer and newer cell phones. When we run out of fuels, we frack rock to extract more, undermining the water sources and foundations of the earth. We move farther and farther away from Eden. When God created humans he didn't place them in a high rise but rather among the hyacinths.

No longer, as Adam and Eve once did, do we hear the sound of the Lord God as He walks in the garden in the cool of the day.

Which is one reason to care for the earth: so that we might fall *toward,* instead of from, grace. In earth care, we reconnect with the memory of Eden, life with God, that is locked deep within our bones and souls, deeper than any genetic code. Caring for instead of raping creation reconnects us with the eternal, ongoing presence of Divine life.

Quaker Audrey Urry said:

> All species and the Earth itself have interdependent roles within Creation.…All parts, all issues, are inextricably intertwined. Indeed the web of creation could be described as of three-ply thread: wherever we touch it we affect justice and peace and the health of all everywhere. So all our testimonies, all our Quaker work, all our Quaker lives are part of one process, of striving towards a flourishing, just and peaceful Creation—the Kingdom of God.

The perfect garden. Our souls contain a spiritual seed of longing for the perfection of that place. We can put our hearts and minds and bodies to work restoring God's green earth.

Thus endeth the bad Quaker's sermon.

CHAPTER 7
WALKING CHEERFULLY

A Little Levity Never Hurt Anybody (Well, Except for That One Guy)

Be patterns, be examples in all countries, places, islands, nations, wherever you come, that your carriage and life may preach among all sorts of people, and to them; then you will come to walk cheerfully over the world, answering that of God in every one.
—George Fox

In his cool sunglasses
And his bright Hawaiian shirt
Foxy George is telling Friends
A little fun won't hurt.
—Gretta Stone

You filter out an ant but swallow a camel.
—Jesus

Seriousness is the only refuge of the shallow.
—Oscar Wilde

One day, when I was an executive at a not-for-profit organization, I received a package from Oregon. It was from my friend Howard Macy (you'll hear more about him). Opening it I found a presentation box containing a booklet entitled *The Red Nose Training Manual* and two red foam clown noses. Now I've rarely been accused of being too serious, but this Red Nose humor called for a different slant than my usual sly self is used to. The nose is about being in a spirit of fun. So, even though I was at work, I popped it on the end of my nose for the rest of that day and here's what I found.

- It's hard to read a computer screen with a big, red, out-of-focus blob moving around where you're trying to look.
- It's also hard to drink water.
- It's even harder to act as if work decisions are life-and-death while discussing them with colleagues when you're wearing a big red nose.
- People you think would stop in their tracks when they see you wearing a big red nose often don't miss a beat and walk on by (often whilst muttering some comment like "I always knew you were a Bozo"). Others, though, just stop and stare and can't find anything to say, so walk on.
- Strangers passing you on the street want to look at you but won't (at least here in the Midwest—that politeness thing, I guess) and so are really obvious about trying to look elsewhere. But they keep stealing glances.
- Clothes don't make the man—the nose makes the man. A fine, grey, window-pane, wool-cashmere suit, freshly ironed dress shirt, and beautiful silk tie become invisible if you're wearing a clown nose.
- Nothing you wear or do surprises your spouse.
- Wearing a clown nose, after the initial self-consciousness wears off, is actually very freeing and relaxing.

I made that last discovery while wearing the nose through rush-hour traffic on the way home. It's normally a very uptight time for me—people are always getting in my way (how dare they!), going slow in the speed lane, cutting in front of me, tailgating me, pushing me to push the speed limit. But, with the clown nose on, I found myself slowing down, allowing people to zoom by, cut in, change lanes without signaling, and various other annoying things without getting all upset by it. It's hard to get bent out of shape when your face is already bent out of shape! It's hard to glare at somebody while wearing a big red nose. In fact, the nose enlarged my soul for that period that I wore it.

> *Silly shows us our true place in this life: we are not the center of the universe.*

That sounds silly, I know, but I think that's the point. The silly shows us our true place in this life: we are not the center of the universe, though, as *The Red Nose Training Manual* says, we can see it from where we are. The silly says, *Slow down, enjoy, be kind, be caring, be not-caring about yourself, and smile on the outside and the inside. Trust God.*

And that's all the nose from my hometown.

QUICK QUAKER QUESTIONS

Remember, no one right answer. What's your soul say?

- When is the last time I really had a good laugh—a laugh that fed my spirit?

Stumbles in Bad Quaker History: Take My Wife ... Please

At one point in our history, Quakers "disowned" from membership Friends who did things disapproved by the community. This included marrying someone who was not a Quaker. William Rathbone V, onetime mayor of Liverpool, England, and a prominent merchant, found himself disowned for marrying a Unitarian. He was readmitted to membership after he told his meeting that, out of courtesy to his wife, he could not say he repented of marrying "out-of-meeting," but he could say he wouldn't do it again.

STUMBLING SEMISERIOUSLY OVER THE WORLD

George Fox, as you just read, once said, "Walk cheerfully over the world, answering that of God in everyone." We Friends are pretty good at the second part of that suggestion but often could use some work on the first. Which is just one reason that I appreciate my friend Howard. A serious (in a good way) biblical scholar, Howard continually reminds us that cheerlessness is not next to godliness. In fact, it's nearly impossible to be godly if one is not cheerful. Remember, even mostly dour Saint Paul thought cheerfulness was a good thing—"God loves a cheerful giver." I'd have been happy if he used some other noun than "giver," though. How about "God loves a cheerful *liver*" or "God loves a cheerful bad Quaker" or something along those lines?

As a renowned scholar, Howard offers wonderfully accessible analyses of the uses of humor in the Bible. And that's no joke. We rarely think of Scripture as a source of knee-slappers. I mean, just look at Elijah's poking fun at the prophets of Baal—"Shout louder!" he said. "Surely he is a god! Perhaps he is deep in thought, or busy, or traveling. Maybe he is sleeping and must be awakened." Especially sarcastic is the "deep in thought" part, where it implies he might be off on a different sorta throne doing…um…his business. The Bible is filled with stories of trickery, talking animals, and proverbs with an edge (check out Proverbs 27:15).

Jesus, whose ministry was of a most serious nature, knew the power of humor and irony. Why else would He tell a story about a camel going through the eye of a needle? Every schoolchild, regardless of theologians and biblical historians trying to explain what He really meant, knows that camels can't fit through needle eyes. It's funny even to try to picture it. The absurdity of the situation is what drove Jesus' point home to the people who were listening to Him. That was part of His healing ministry. Healing the rift between the moral ideal and actual behavior, sinner and saint, sickness and wellness, God and man was all made easier with humor.

What's most helpful about much of what Howard writes reminds us that the biblical stories are about, and meant for, people like us. "The Bible is often funny, just as we should expect it to be," writes Howard, "if it truly reflects the full range of faith and life." He loves to point out the Bibles' jokes, riddles, comic stories, satire, and word play.

Okay, so the Bible is full of humor. So what? What does that have to do with my life? Well, for one, it encourages me in my love of humor. While many of the Quaker saints I know are still hoping I'll grow up and quit being such a smart aleck, Howard reminds me (and you) that our spiritual journeys have "to do with all of life, not just with conse- crated chunks set off in a corner.... If Brother Lawrence could expe- rience God fully while peeling potatoes, perhaps we can learn to love God amid peals of laughter."

Phew. After all, lots of life is just plain funny. Especially if you're semi-accident prone like I am. I mean, all the wacky things that have happened to me while trying to be a farmer tell me that God has to have a sense of humor. Why else would God stick me—a man who loves big cities and riding the commuter train—on a fifty-acre farm in the mid- dle of nowhere? Especially when you add in the Brent Bill Klutz Factor. I can imagine the heavenly host gathering around anytime I fire up the tractor. "What's he going to run into today?" "Bet he breaks his glasses and gets a black eye." "How about we get a limb to knock a lens out of his glasses? Then he could get off his tractor to look for it. He could take off the glasses so he could look closely at the ground, find the lens, put it safe in his coverall pockets, and then drive over the glasses he left on the ground!" "Oh, he wouldn't do that." "Just watch!"

I mean, I'm so far from *ept* around here that even I have to laugh. Once the swelling goes down.

QUICK QUAKER QUESTIONS

Remember, no one right answer. What's your soul say?

- Has there ever been a time I was ever tempted to laugh at something in the Bible?
- At what? And why?

HOLY HILARITY

"Humor can be dissected, as a frog can," said E. B. White, "but the thing dies in the process and the innards are discouraging to any but the pure scientific mind." That being the case, I don't want to dissect humor much further—other than to say that there are, in the Quaker experience, some things that make for good humor. And some that don't.

One thing is to think who the target of the humor is—and isn't. Most good Quaker humor, even by bad Quakers, is self-directed. Humor can really wound when directed at others—ethnic groups, people with religions other than our own, political parties. Even more, it can wound us, by making us smaller than we would want to be. Humor directed at others is often hateful or hostile—look at the Elijah story I just mentioned.

Besides, we have enough failings ourselves! Plenty of material to work from. When Jacob Stone and I started the Association of Bad Friends, it was because we were sitting around joking about all the quirks we Quakers had. We didn't need to go outside the fold to find funny fodder—our mangers were full of it.

That's why most Quaker humor is about ourselves and our queer ways. Our jokes tend to be along the following lines:

Q: How many Quakers does it take to change a lightbulb?
A: None. Who needs to change a bulb when we have the Inner Light?
(Or)
A: Thirty-four. One to raise a concern at Ministry and Counsel that the lightbulb is no longer working. Ten at Ministry and Counsel to name Friends to serve on a lightbulb replacement subgroup to send a report to Monthly Meeting. Three to work on the subgroup and report to Monthly Meeting. Fifteen at Monthly Meeting to discern that the right way forward is to change the lightbulb. One to report back to Ministry and Counsel that the bulb is going to be changed. One Friend to change the bulb. One Quaker to write an article for the Meeting's newsletter about the changing of the bulb. One to write a letter of complaint to *Friends Journal* saying that the decision about changing the lightbulb had not been in Right Ordering.

Q. How do Friends start a race?
A. Ready...set...go when the Spirit moves you!

Q. What do you get when you cross a Quaker with a Jehovah's Witness?
A. Someone who knocks on your door and then stands there saying absolutely nothing.

Jacob and I even came up with this little gadget:

New from Bill Stone Enterprises! It's Ye Olde Quaker Whoopee Cushion, the fun product made with Friends in mind. Slip an Olde Quaker Whoopee Cushion under the bench pad at Meeting and watch the Friends quake. When a weighty Friend plops his backside down, out comes the sound of silence. Imagine the look on the Meeting folks' faces!

The Olde Quaker Whoopee Cushion is perfect for unprogrammed and programmed Friends alike. Its one size fits all shapes, works on benches, pews, pulpit furniture, choir chairs, and more.

It comes in grey or gray.

And it's only $19.95 plus postage and handling.

But wait. Order in the next twenty minutes and we'll throw in another Olde Quaker Whoopee Cushion at no extra cost. And that's not all! The first twenty callers will receive a copy of *Walk Cheerfully: The George Fox Jokebook.*

Just call 1-666-QUAKER. Operators are standing by.

Quick Quaker Questions

Remember, no one right answer. What's your soul say?

- What about my faith do I find amusing? What makes me laugh—secretly, if not aloud? Or allowed? Why?

Stumbles in Bad Quaker History: A Quiet Quaker Wife

John Salkeld, an eighteenth-century Quaker, was visited by the elders of his meeting because they felt he joked too much. The elders stayed and stayed at his home, laboring (as they used to say) with him about his excessive use of humor. At one point, Salkeld went into the kitchen and returned, exclaiming, "Friends, come at once. My wife is speechless." The elders hurried into the kitchen and found Salkeld's wife—asleep.

A Spirit of Fun

The Quaker way is in no small part about living in a spirit of fun and cultivating a joyful attitude in the midst of family, work, and all our other personal and communal activity. We profess a faith that is cause for great rejoicing. We need to let that joyfulness find its way to our faces now and then. We need to be careful that we do not take the business of worship, church, and life so seriously that we look as if we've been sucking on lemons most of our lives.

A good laugh keeps us from becoming super-sanctimonious, self-righteous hypocrites who scare others away from the good news of God's healing and saving love. Laughter leads us out of the overbearing seriousness of a situation and helps us see the silly positions we place ourselves in at times. It is a wonderful release and a tonic for the ails of everyday life.

Erasmus wrote:

> No morons so play the fool as those who are obsessed with the ardor of Christian piety to the point they...eschew pleasure, glut themselves

with...vigils [and] tears as if the soul lived elsewhere and not in the body. What is this if not insanity. No wonder that the apostles appeared to be drunk with new wine and Paul seemed to Festus to be mad. "For God has chosen the foolish things of the world to confound the wise and the weak things of the world to confound the mighty."

He wrote this in a piece entitled *The Praise of Folly*.

We will "come to walk cheerfully over the world, answering that of God in every man [and woman]." We know that is true when we do something as simple as smile at someone we meet at a mall or are shopping next to in the supermarket. There is something down deep that responds to the gesture of a friendly smile from the heart. A ministry of mirth.

To walk cheerfully. What a joyous command. It helps us realize that our faith in Christ is meant to bring happiness and rejoicing, not despair and gloom. It is a call to the goodness of God and an enjoyment of His creation.

> *To walk cheerfully. What a joyous command.*

Let us learn to rejoice in the Lord at all times. We need to learn to enjoy ourselves, even as our Lord enjoys us.

Say, did you hear the one...

QUICK QUAKER QUESTIONS

Remember, no one right answer. What's your soul say?

- How might I live more in a spirit of holy hilarity? Or at least a bit less seriously?

I saw, out of the corner of my eye, something fly by my office door, screeching as it went. At the time, I was in charge of personnel and maintaining corporate discipline at a serious-minded, religious not-for-profit. So, more than a bit startled, I went to see what it was when another zoomed by, howling as it went. It was an Amazing Flying Monkey. Yikes!

One thing you need to know about me is that I don't like screechy, flying things (hmmm, that could be a description of me in an airplane). I've been especially afraid of flying monkeys ever since I was a kid, thanks to those evil critters in *The Wizard of Oz*.

In this case, these "super stretchy screaming monkeys" were a lunchtime purchase by my friend Nancy. She had brought them back to the office and was launching them like slingshots down the hall. Soon, others were joining in—including me. So much for corporate discipline. Indeed, after sufficient whining on my part, Nancy gave me one of my very own to keep.

Nancy had become quite adept at shooting them and hers traveled a long way, screeching the whole time. One was shot (not by me) into Aaron's office—it fell howling into the space of no return between his desk and the wall. The launcher had to retrieve it with a set of salad tongs from the kitchen. Then Aaron locked his office door. Tim, our leader, just came out of his office, shook his head, and went back to work. Isn't dignified for the president to consort with monkey-launchers, I guess.

Besides the screaming of the airborne primates, the main sound was laughter. Giggles. Guffaws. Belly laughs. It was just so silly.

It was, of course, inevitable that somebody would get hurt. I could almost hear Santa Claus in *A Christmas Story* saying, "You'll shoot your eye out, kid." No one's eye got put out—instead the tail of my monkey tore off as I was launching him. Poor monkey. I didn't know whether to take him back to the toy store and ask for another or not. Seemed a bit of a silly thing for an almost fifty-nine-year-old man to do. "May I have another flying monkey, please?" So my friend Nancy did it for me.

My standing there with a monkey tail in one hand and a screaming monkey stuck on the fingers of my other hand was a source of great amusement to the others, though.

It was good to laugh. Really good. Just-what-I-needed good.

As I laughed, I thought about how God wants us to enjoy life. I didn't ponder it a long time—seemed as though it would be counterproductive to get ultraserious about how God likes us to laugh. But I did remember a verse from Nehemiah 8: " 'Go, eat rich food, and drink something sweet,' he said to them, 'and send portions of this to any who have nothing ready! This day is holy to our Lord. Don't be sad, because the joy from the Lord is your strength!' "

Ah, a little choice food (like maybe a filet mignon), a little wine (Côtes du Rhône would be nice), and a screaming flying monkey or two. Rejoice. Rejoice in the Lord always.

CHAPTER 8

CLOSING DEEP THOUGHTS...

And a Word on Fashion

To be a friend of God: that's the essence of the Quaker way. "You are my friends," as Jesus said. Even if, at times, we're not very good at being the kind of friends we'd like to be. Still, the tenets of Quaker faith and practice invite us to live with spiritual imagination, so that every step we take brings us closer to God and is a creative act. That's where we get the cheerfulness that George Fox talked about.

Faith is a great frontier to explore. God's Spirit calls to us to look deep in our souls. So we try to heed that call and live out our faith daily whether we walk the high wire strung between life's chasms or the gentle path beside the still waters. The more we walk in God's way, with Divine assistance, the better we get at being fully human. A large part of learning to walk with God is learning to listen for the Divine in daily life and to look for traces of the Spirit as we go. That's the wisdom of the Quaker way—a wisdom that cuts across denominational and faith lines. God calls us all to be his friends—not just the Friends! We are all called to live in the way of wholeness and holiness.

As we learn to carry stillness with us, move more deeply into lives of peace, equality, simplicity, etc., we find that they don't drain our spirits or render us humorless or unfit for human company. Instead we find that they bring us to a new place of joy because we have moved into our rightful place as God's friends. We experience the rejuvenation of our spirits that occurs when we listen for, to, and with God. **Our lives begin to demonstrate fully the values and beliefs we hold most dear.** We find ourselves not only blessed with personal fulfillment, but with a deeper communion with God and others.

As we do so, we learn ways of walking cheerfully through life no matter its circumstances. To do so is not to deny the reality of pain and sadness in our lives, but to acknowledge that we are learning to live more fully in God's presence, a place of love and joy and peace. The more we develop the art of soulful living, the more we can rejoice in the Light—because God is with us. God's joy and peace permeate our lives so much that they then ripple out into the world in a "paying it forward" sort of way.

The essence of being friends with God is that we are on a continual journey to goodness and fulfillment. It is not that we achieve sainthood suddenly. Obviously, I haven't. Rather it's about realizing that, with God's assistance, we move deeper into walking so close to God that we live as the fullest possible human beings. Being friends with God calls us to our best selves—and lives of soulful satisfaction.

Thus endeth the sermon of the leader of the Bad Friends.

Oh, that's right. I almost forgot. I promised a word about fashion. Here it is: khakis.

APPENDIX 1

HUMBLE STUMBLE HYMNBOOK: SPIRITUAL SONGS FOR IMPERFECT SAINTS

Music has always played a big role in my spiritual life (guess that's obvious from all the LPs, CDs, cassettes, and MP3s I've admitted I have). I often listen to tunes, too, when I'm writing. So it seemed like a good idea when I began writing this little book to create a soundtrack for it. That evolved into a project on my blog (holyordinary.blogspot.com) and Spotify that I call the *Humble Stumble Hymnbook*. Below are fifteen of my favorite hymns from the hymnal.

This collection is composed of songs that have spoken to my soul in a spiritual sense even if they are not "spiritual songs" per se. They are not hymns in the traditional sense. Rather they're songs I chose based on my bias that our hearts hunger for beauty and meaning and so when artists create something that sings deep in our souls, well, they've created a hymn, even if they did so unintentionally.

I continually add new "hymns" and you're welcome to check them out on Spotify or the blog. Just search *Humble Stumble Hymnbook*. When it's possible, I post the lyrics and a video, too, as well as a link to the artist's website. You're welcome to send suggestions for the hymnbook based on what songs speak deeply to your soul.

Humble Stumble Hymnbook:
Spiritual Songs for Imperfect Saints

Hymns of Hope and Blessing

"A Light in the Window" by Carrie Newcomer. "I can see a light / There's a light in the window."

"Seven Angels" by Hem. "Sleep come easy to your bed this night / Seven angels hold you in their light."

Hymns for the Family of God

"All My Favorite People" by Over the Rhine. "All my favorite people are broken."

"City of Immigrants" by Steve Earle. "All of us are immigrants / Every daughter, every son."

"Mercyland" by Phil Madeira. "So let's you and me take each other's hand / let's travel on down, down to Mercyland."

Hymns of Affirmation

"Good Light" by Drew Holcomb and The Neighbors. "Hey, there's a good light, shining in you."

"I Know I'm Not Alone" by Michael Franti. "I know I'm far away from home but I know I'm not alone."

Hymns of Repentance and Obedience

"If Only Avenue" by Ron Sexsmith. "It's strange, as people we're prone to dwell / On things that we can't undo."

"Show Me the Place" by Leonard Cohen. "Show me the place, help me roll away the stone."

Hymns of Aspiration

"The Gospel of Carlos, Norman and Smith" by Rickie Lee Jones. "I keep trying to believe in believing."

"When Will I Ever Learn to Live in God?" by Van Morrison. "When will I ever learn to live in God? / When will I ever learn?"

Hymns of Peace

"With God on Our Side" by Buddy Miller. "If God's on our side / He'll stop the next war."

"Holy Wars and Politicians" by Jan Krist. "Save us all from Holy wars and politicians."

Hymns of Praise

"Hymn" by Peter, Paul and Mary. "All that I could say was I believe in You."

"Rebel Jesus" by Jackson Browne. "On the side of the rebel Jesus."

APPENDIX 2

THE GOOD, THE BAD, AND THE QUAKERS

A number of famous or infamous figures are Quakers or have a Friends background or connections. I'll leave it up to you to decide which category (good or bad) those on the short list below belong in. I've omitted the names of any Friends, good or bad, who have already been mentioned in the book.

Jane Addams (1860–1935) worked for women's rights and pioneered the American settlement house movement at Hull House in Chicago.

Susan B. Anthony (1820–1906) was an abolitionist and women's rights activist.

Edmund Bacon (1910–2005) was a prominent architect and onetime executive director of the Philadelphia City Planning Commission. He was the father of actor Kevin Bacon, thus enabling the game Six Degrees of Kevin Bacon.

Joan Baez (1941–) is a social activist and musician, credited with more than thirty albums.

Daniel Boone (1734–1820) was an American frontiersman who blazed the Wilderness Trail through the Cumberland Gap in what is now Kentucky. His descendant Pat Boone sang the theme song of the 1956 film *Friendly Persuasion* about Civil War–era Quakers in Indiana. The song was nominated for an Academy Award.

Jorge Luis Borges (1899–1986) was an Argentine short story writer, poet, essayist, and translator.

Sandra Boynton (1953–) is best known as a cartoonist and illustrator. She is also an author with more than fifty books for both children and adults.

Jocelyn Bell Burnell (1943–) is an astrophysicist who, as a graduate student, was the first to discover radio pulsars.

A. S. Byatt (1936–) is a writer who won the Man Booker Prize for her novel *Possession*, which was also made into a film.

David Byrne (1952–) of the Talking Heads also works in film and theater.

James Fennimore Cooper (1789–1851) was a writer most famous today for his novel *The Deerslayer* and his character Natty Bumpo.

Cassius Coolidge (1844–1934) was an artist who is best known today for his paintings of dogs playing poker.

Ezra Cornell (1807–1874) founded Western Union and Cornell University.

James Dean (1931–1955) was an actor (appearing in three films) whose untimely death in an automobile accident turned him into a pop icon and the example of "cool."

Jack Larson (1928–) is an actor with more than twenty movie credits, but he is best known as cub reporter Jimmy Olsen in 1950s television series *The Adventures of Superman*.

Caleb Deschanel (1944–) is an award-winning American cinematographer and the father of actresses Zooey Deschanel and Emily Deschanel.

Fritz Eichenberg (1901–1990) was an illustrator best known for his black-and-white wood prints, many of which have a social justice theme. He was a close friend of Dorothy Day.

Sam Harris (1967–) is one of the New Atheists and the author of *The End of Faith: Religion, Terror, and the Future of Reason*.

Jan de Hartog (1914–2002) was a Dutch-born playwright, novelist, and social critic. He won a Tony award for his play *The Fourposter*.

Edward Hicks (1780–1849) was one of the first "primitive" American painters—at a time when Quakers disapproved of the arts.

Charles Elmer Hires (1851–1937) was a Philadelphia pharmacist who developed commercial root beer.

Herbert Hoover (1874–1964) was a mining engineer who rose to international prominence due to his directing humanitarian relief efforts in World War I–era Belgium. He later became president of the United States.

Johns Hopkins (1795–1873) was an abolitionist, entrepreneur, and philanthropist whose bequests founded a number of institutions bearing his name.

Haven Kimmel (1965–) is a *New York Times* best-selling author of a number of novels and memoirs, including *A Girl Named Zippy: Growing Up Small in Mooreland, Indiana.*

Ben Kingsley (1943–) was born Krishna Pandit Bhanji and is a versatile actor who has played heroes (Gandhi), villains (a hit man with a drinking problem), and everything in between.

Eric Knight (1897–1943) was an English-born novelist and children's writer best known today for *Lassie Come-Home.*

Lyndon LaRouche (1922–) is a radical, controversial American politician and pundit.

David Lean (1908–1991) was a British film director who is best known today for epics such as *Doctor Zhivago, Lawrence of Arabia,* and *The Bridge on the River Kwai.*

Dolley Madison (1768–1849) was the first Quaker first lady of the United States.

Dave Matthews (1967–) is a musician. The Dave Matthews Band sold more tickets and earned more money than any other act in North America in 2000–2010.

James Michener (1907–1997) was a philanthropist and an author famous for epic novels such as *Alaska, Chesapeake, Centennial,* and more. His *Tales of the South Pacific* won the Pulitzer Prize and was adapted into a musical.

Elizabeth Magie (1866–1948) was a game inventor who designed The Landlord's Game to illustrate the economic ills of land monopolies. The game is now known as Monopoly.

Edward R. Murrow (1908–1965) was a pioneering journalist on early television whose reports helped lead to the censure of Red Scare senator Joseph McCarthy.

Carrie Newcomer (I asked her birth year. She says she forgets) is a singer-songwriter, social activist, and cultural ambassador.

Samuel Nicholas (1744–1790) was the first commander of the United States Marine Corps.

Annie Oakley (1860–1926) was born Phoebe Ann Mosey and was known as a sharpshooter and star of Wild West shows in the late nineteenth and early twentieth centuries.

Parker Palmer (1939–) is an educator, spiritual and political activist, and author, notably of *Let Your Life Speak: Listening for the Voice of Vocation*.

Bonnie Raitt (1949–) is an influential singer and musician with ten Grammy awards.

Betsy Ross (1752–1836) is credited with creating the first American flag.

Bayard Rustin (1912–1987) was a US civil rights leader whose Quaker values, especially regarding nonviolence, influenced the direction of Martin Luther King Jr. and his work to end segregation, poverty, and war.

Joan Slonczewski (1956–) is a professor of biology and science fiction writer. Two of her books have earned the John W. Campbell Memorial Award for Best Science Fiction Novel.

Edwin Stanton (1814–1869) was a politician who served as United States secretary of war under Presidents Lincoln and Johnson.

Joseph H. Taylor (1941–) is an astrophysicist and cowinner of the 1993 Nobel Prize in Physics.

Henry S. Taylor (1942–) is a poet and winner of the 1986 Pulitzer Prize for poetry.

Cheryl Tiegs (1947–) is the only supermodel known to have Quaker connections.

Walt Whitman (1819–1892) was one of the preeminent American poets of his time.

Benjamin West (1738–1820) was an artist contemporary of fellow Quaker artist Edward Hicks, but West's works are much more refined and attuned to the English model of painting of the time.

Jessamyn West (1902–1984) was a novelist, short story writer, and screenwriter. She is most famous for her book *Friendly Persuasion*, which was turned into a major film. She also wrote the script for the film. She was a cousin to Richard M. Nixon.

John Greenleaf Whittier (1807–1892) was, like his contemporary Walt Whitman, a major poet. The two did not appreciate each other's work.

John Wimber (1934–1997) was a charismatic spiritual leader and one of the founders of the Vineyard Movement.

APPENDIX 3

WANNA LEARN MORE?

I hope you've found this book entertaining, engaging, and helpful as you think about how to be a little bit better at being good—and maybe not so bad at...um...not being good. I've tried to give you a glimpse of how, for more than 350 years, the Quaker way has helped people live more fully as the people they'd like to be. But this book provides only a glimpse. If you'd like to know more about the Quaker ways of silence, peace, and equality, there are a number of other books you might want to look at.

As a Bad Quaker, I am, of course, first going to recommend my own! Reviewers and people who read them think they're pretty good—and, besides, I need the money. These volumes are not quite as humorous as this book—but they are, if I may say, wise, winsome, and invitational.

Holy Silence: The Gift of Quaker Spirituality (Paraclete Press, 2005). A book that shares how Quakers use sacramental silence as a tool to deeper faith and communion with God. You will learn ways of implementing this holy silence more fully into your faith life.

Mind the Light: Learning to See with Spiritual Eyes (Paraclete Press, 2006). This little book invites you to see with spiritual eyes both your inner and outer lives. This book is about two things—minding the Light and learning to look. It explores where in our lives light switches may be found and how minding the Light leads us closer to God and God's creation.

Sacred Compass: The Way of Spiritual Discernment (Paraclete Press, 2008). A compass makes a good metaphor for our spiritual lives and the work of discerning God's will for them since God doesn't speak through MapQuest, GoogleMaps, or GPS. Keeping our souls' eyes on the sacred compass leads us to the holy discovery that we can move through life with purpose and promise, even when we may not sense with certainty what that purpose and promise are. As we move toward Divine guidance, we joyfully behold the face of a loving God gazing back at us.

Awaken Your Senses: Exercises for Exploring the Wonder of God (cowritten with Beth A. Booram) (IVP, 2012). This is a book where you don't just read about meeting God through your senses of touch, smell, taste, hearing, and seeing. Instead, you have experiences that are highly sensory and participatory. The content uses artistic elements, contemplative exercises, and engaging interaction with the text, the arts, and your five senses.

Finding God in the Verbs: Crafting a Fresh Language of Prayer (cowritten with Jennie Isbell) (IVP, 2015). Many of us say the same prayers over and over again. This book is about expanding our prayer language and our prayers so that we might more completely connect with God. It shows us how to develop a fresh way of seeing God, ourselves, and our relationship with God through words that really matter to us.

Okay, so much for shameless shelf (as in bookshelf) promotion. Here are some other recommendations.

BOOKS

A Testament of Devotion by Thomas Kelly (Harper, 1941). A classic of Quaker spirituality, centering on cultivating an inner life of worship, holy obedience, and practical spirituality in daily life.

Letters to a Fellow Seeker by Steve Chase (QuakerBooks of FGC, 2012). This uses fictional correspondence between an experienced Friend and a spiritual seeker to introduce the Quaker way in a powerful but personal way.

Peace Be with You: A Study of the Spiritual Basis of the Friends Peace Testimony by Sandra Cronk (Tract Association of Friends, 1984). A little booklet that is chock-full of information about why the peaceful way is a spiritual way rooted in the Gospel of Jesus. Available online at http://www.tractassociation.org/pamphlets/peace-you-study-spiritual-basis-friends-peace-testimony/.

Silence and Witness: The Quaker Tradition by Michael Birkel (Orbis, 2004). This gives a good in-depth look at Quaker worship, the inward life, and doing discernment the Quaker way.

The Quakers: A Very Short Introduction by Pink Dandelion (Oxford University Press, 2008). A marvelous overview of Quaker life today by one of the people leading the revitalization of the Friends message for today.

WEBSITES

Friends General Conference features a good many materials that offer information about Quakers today—including the QuakerFinder, where you can locate Friends close to you in case you'd like to visit one of our meetings. http://www.fgcquaker.org/.

The Tract Association of Friends offers a number of resources (many of which are free) on a wide range of topics related to Quaker faith and practice. http://www.tractassociation.org/.

Voices of Friends is a place to learn more about Quakers around the world. It has reading materials (including some in Spanish); a library of blogs, websites, online materials, and more. http://www.voicesoffriends.org/index.php.

Warning: While I've admitted that I am the "leader" of the Association of Bad Friends on Facebook (and you're welcome to check it out at https://www.facebook.com/groups/assbadfriends/), that group does not have a website. If you Google Bad Quakers, you will be given the listing for an anarchist site that has nothing to do with Quakers.

APPENDIX 4

SOME GOOD ADVICES:

Friendly Food for Faith and Thought

Take heed, dear Friends, to the promptings of love and truth in your hearts. Trust them as the leadings of God whose Light shows us our darkness and brings us to new life. —Advice #1 in Quaker faith & practice: The book of Christian discipline of the Yearly Meeting of the Religious Society of Friends (Quakers) in Britain

Quakers, being a non-credal people, don't have doctrinal statements to point to or many theological tomes in which we search for guidance. Instead, we rely on the Holy Spirit speaking in our souls, searching scripture, and the collective spiritual wisdom of our faith community. Much of this collective wisdom has been collected in what we call Faith and Practice, a Friendly sort of book of discipline. The best ones gather the experiences of Friends in their own words and make them available for us to learn from today. Another section in most Faith and Practices is one called "Advices," which are statements that urge Friends to

The following are not (for the most part) formal "Advices," but they are advices from (mostly) good Friends past and present who have lived the spiritual life fully and well. I encourage you to Google these Friends. Their lives were and are fascinating and inspirational. Fortunately for us, they all have shared some of their wisdom for our edification.

Some of the things collected here are prayers. Some are poems. Some are brief thoughts about, as Quakers say, "that which is eternal." All of them are food for spiritual growth.

Too many times we pray for ease, but that's a prayer seldom met. What we need to do is pray for roots that reach deep into the Eternal, so when the rains fall and the winds blow, we won't be swept asunder. —Philip J. Gulley

**

There is a spirit which I feel that delights to do no evil, nor to revenge any wrong, but delights to endure all things, in hope to enjoy its own in the end. Its hope is to outlive all wrath and contention, and to weary out all exaltation and cruelty, or whatever is of a nature contrary to itself. It sees to the end of all temptations. As it bears no evil in itself, so it conceives none in thoughts to any other. If it be betrayed, it bears it, for its ground and spring is the mercies and forgiveness of God. Its crown is meekness, its life is everlasting love unfeigned; and takes its kingdom with entreaty and not with contention, and keeps it by lowliness of mind. —James Nayler (1616–1660)

**

Words may help and silence may help, but the one thing needful is that the heart should turn to its Maker as the needle turns to the pole. For this we must be still. —Caroline Stephen (1834–1909)

**

Inner silence, calming the agitations of our hearts and minds, letting go of all that is stubborn and grasping, is essentially an expression of the love of truth. To be dispassionate, not to let one's own needs or prejudices or emotions color one's actions, is essentially to put truth before everything else. To love truth in this way is to love God, who is Truth. Thus the practice of inner silence is the same as the love of God. —Dan Seeger

***

The likeness we bear to Jesus is more essential than our notions of him. —Lucretia Mott (1793–1880)

***

The discovery of God lies in the daily and the ordinary, not in the spectacular and the heroic. If we cannot find God in the routines of home and shop, then we will not find Him at all. —Richard J. Foster

***

Friends come back from their worship with a new sense of ordination, but not the ordination of human hands. Something has happened in the stillness that makes the heart more tender, more sensitive, more shocked by evil, more dedicated to ideals of life, and more eager to push back the skirts of darkness and to widen the area of light and love. — Rufus Jones (1863–1948)

***

Contemporary Christians find that they face many of the same questions as the early hermits. How does one find one's true self? How can we learn to see what is illusory and what is real? How do certain elements in our society's value structure block our ability to hear God's call? What does it mean to live a life of prayer? How can we find a firm foundation on which to build our lives? —Sandra Cronk (1942–2000)

***

To me, being a Christian is a particular way of life... being the kind of person that Jesus wanted his followers to be and doing the things he told them to do.... Nor, it seems to me, can you live a Christian life unless, like Jesus, you believe in the power of goodness, of mercy and of love. —Kathleen Lonsdale (1903–1971)

***

What is the Quaker faith? It is not a tidy package of words which you can capture at any given time and then repeat weekly at a worship service. It is an experience of discovery which starts the discoverer on a journey which is life-long. The discovery in itself is not uniquely a property of Quakerism. It is as old as Christianity, and considerably older if you share the belief that many have known Christ who have not known His name. What is unique to the Religious Society of Friends is its insistence that the discovery must be made by each man for himself. No one is allowed to get it second-hand by accepting a ready-made creed. Furthermore, the discovery points a path and demands a journey, and gives you the power to make the journey. —Elise Boulding (1920–2010)

***

The one cornerstone of belief upon which the Society of Friends is built is the conviction that God does indeed communicate with each one of the spirits He has made, in a direct and living inbreathing of some measure of the breath of His own Life; that He never leaves Himself without a witness in the heart as well as in the surroundings of man; that the measure of light, life, or grace thus given increases by obedience; and that in order clearly to hear the Divine voice speaking within us we need to be still; to be alone with Him, in the secret place of His Presence; that all flesh should keep silence before Him. —Caroline Stephen (1834–1909)

***

From this fog-bound Earth of ours
We take refuge in you.
O rest of our souls,
Escaping like birds from a broken cage
To the keen, clear air, and the sunny uplands
Where you dwell, and with you
Find release from meanness of spirit,
From jealousy, slander, hypocrisy,
From selfish ambition,
From the insidious darkness that broods
And breeds in our wills and hides
The vision of good and the pathway of peace.
We take refuge in you:
Let us walk honestly in the daylight.
—John S. Hoyland (1830–1894)

***

Our life is love, and peace, and tenderness; and bearing one with another, and forgiving one another, and not laying accusations one against another; but praying one for another, and helping one another up with a tender hand. —Isaac Penington (1616-1679)

***

If fighting is inconsistent with an ideal society, then fighting will not bring the ideal society. A spiritual result is produced by spiritual means and a material result by material means. If war is evil, as almost everyone admits, then it cannot be the right way to produce a good result. —Howard Brinton (1884–1973)

***

Only the inner vision of God, only the God-blindedness of unreservedly dedicated souls, only the utterly humble ones can bow and break the raging pride of a power-mad world. —Thomas R Kelly (1893–1941)

***

Quakers are not "for peace" but rather know, in the deepest sense of the word, that peace is a holy imperative as part of a just society. —Ben Pink Dandelion

***

The moral man is he who is opposed to injustice per se, opposed to injustice wherever he finds it; the moral man looks for injustice first of all in himself. —Bayard Rustin (1912–1987)

***

Quaker…"concerns" are usually personal, tested by meetings at different levels, and often lead to specific action. "Testimonies" are more widely shared and accepted, and the sort of action they lead to should affect our whole lives. The essential quality of both is an inner compulsion, not something you decide on after reading or hearing about it. They have that quality of Luther's famous statement "here I stand, I cannot do otherwise." —Tim Brown

***

Eternal God, let thy spirit inspire and guide us. Thy will be done. Give us the strength to fulfill our task without selfishness, slothfulness, or cowardice. Give us the strength to withstand temptations, and to forgive others as we would wish them freely to forgive us. Enable us to repay those who offend us only by redoubling our endeavors never to offend others. Eternal God, we will listen to thy call and obey it in order that we may hear it ever more clearly. Give us the honesty to examine our own acts and thoughts as scrupulously and severely as those of others.... Teach us compassion and enable us to make a real effort to relieve the sufferings of others. Give us the quiet courage needed in all circumstances, and natural to whoever has consecrated his life to thee.... Do not let any defeat, any fall or backsliding ever separate us from thee; in the midst of our weakness let thy love take hold of us and little by little lift us up to thee. Amen. —Pierre Ceresole (1879–1945)

**

The only way to seek God is to seek God first. Deny the nayward, affirm the yeaward, be true to those stirrings and motions which He starts in us, refuse priority to all else, and be faithful to the sacred. —Jean Toomer (1894–1967)

**

We know that the principles of our faith teach that we can be filled with the same life and power and spirit that produced the prophets and saints of the past, but that knowledge has not made prophets and saints out of us. God waits for us to add to that knowledge the willingness to obey the Light consistently and completely. —Cecil Hinshaw (1911–1982)

**

Dear Lord and Father of mankind,
  Forgive our foolish ways!
  Reclothe us in our rightful mind,

In purer lives Thy service find,
In deeper reverence, praise.
—John Greenleaf Whittier (1807–1892)

***

There is a daily round for beauty as well as for goodness, a world of flowers and books and cinemas and clothes and manners as well as of mountains and masterpieces.... God is in all beauty, not only in the natural beauty of earth and sky, but in all fitness of language and rhythm, whether it describe a heavenly vision or a street fight, a Hamlet or a Falstaff, a philosophy or a joke: in all fitness of line and colour and shade, whether seen in the Sistine Madonna or a child's knitted frock: in all fitness of sound and beat and measure, whether the result be Bach's Passion music or a nursery jingle. The quantity of God, so to speak, varies in the different examples, but His quality of beauty in fitness remains the same. —Caroline C. Graveson

***

We are lured toward truth, beauty, and goodness...the lure is pulling at our hearts like some lucid joy inside every actual occasion and all we have to do is...Say yes. —Haven Kimmel

***

Oh Lord, may I be directed what to do and what to leave undone.
—Elizabeth Fry (1780–1845)

***

To live our faith and not merely proclaim it...we should comfort the afflicted, befriend the lonely, house the homeless, speak the plain truth to all people, refrain from judging others, and never kowtow to the rich. —Scott Russell Sanders

***

First, we all have an inner teacher whose guidance is more reliable than anything we can get from a doctrine, ideology, collective belief system, institution, or leader. Second, we all need other people to invite, amplify, and help us discern the inner teacher's voice —Parker J. Palmer

***

The unity of Christians never did nor ever will or can stand in uniformity of thought and opinion, but in Christian love only. —Thomas Story (1670–1742)

***

A true Friends' meeting for worship drawing individuals with varieties of temperament, talent and background always manages to engender a climate of belonging, of community which is infectious and creative. This experience of "belonging" has remained with me over the years and it has grown both in intensity and universality.... The "giving out" of such a sense of community is the natural witness of a Quaker meeting which has in it the seed of life and creative experience. —Ranjit M Chetsingh

***

A religious awakening which does not awaken the sleeper to love has roused them in vain. —Jessamyn West (1902–1984)

***

It is for this grace that we pray; that we, too, may love to excess even though it may appear foolish in the eyes of the world. —Phyllis Richards (1900–1976)

APPENDIX 5

How to Talk Quaker

A Handy Guide to Quakerese

Dialect—noun, *di·a·lect,* often attributive. *A variety of language whose identity is fixed by a factor other than geography*

Though unrecognized by most linguists, there is a distinct Quaker dialect. It's a dialect that often sounds like English but is laden with meanings that most English speakers cannot decipher. In other words, we talk funny. While there is no distinct universal accent, we have a vocabulary that has developed over our almost four hundred years of history. Almost every Quaker knows them no matter where he or she lives and what language he or she speaks (and, as we Friends are all over the globe, this vocabulary has been translated into many languages).

Below is a list of some of our most well known words or phrases. You might find them interesting. You might even find some you would like to adopt. That's because, while we Quakers are known for truth-telling, we have found ways over the years to say what we think in such a way that offense cannot be taken with the words, but the meaning is clear. Quakerese is a kinder, gentler way of being pacifist-aggressive with our words.

Other Quakerese words or phrases are just helpful at expressing the mystery of some of our encounters with the Divine. They leave room for spiritual exploration and growth. They are an invitation to go deeper in the life of the Spirit.

With a little practice, and with help from the guide below, you too can speak Quakerese like a birthright Friend—to the bemusement and bafflement of your friends.

Approve—how Friends state agreement with a decision in meeting for worship with attention to business (our version of a business meeting). Quakers don't vote. We strive to reach a "sense of the meeting" in regard to what God wants us to do. When the sense of the meeting is read, if we agree that what's been read is the sense of the meeting, we say "Approve."

"I respectfully state that I cannot approve" means "Over my dead body."

"Will thee stand aside, Friend?" is Quakerese for "Will you allow the meeting to proceed with the action it feels is the sense of the meeting?" or, depending on the tone, "Over your dead body."

As (or if) Way Opens—how we say "God willing." Example: "I'll see you at meeting tomorrow as way opens," believing that way will open if God wants me to see you at meeting tomorrow. Of course, that leaves the possibility that way will close (as in I wake up on my deathbed in the morning...or just oversleep, which I take to mean that God knew I needed rest and the alarm didn't go off).

"The meeting will proceed with this project as way opens" also means "We'll move forward when somebody comes through with the cash we need."

Birthright Friend—someone who is born to Quaker parents. The longer the Quaker lineage the more the person can flaunt his or her Friendly pedigree and scowl at remarks by new Friends (which the majority of Quakers today are!).

First Day—the Quaker way of saying Sunday. Early Friends developed what they called "plain speech." Part of plain speech was using numbers for the days and months rather than using the common names that came from non-Christian sources (Thursday or "Thor's day") or were erroneous (December is not the tenth [Dec] month). So plain-speaking Friends call Thursday Fifth Day and December Twelfth Month.

    Most Friends today don't use plain speech except to confuse newcomers or visitors to meeting. It's one way we can let them know that, even though we just became Quakers ourselves a month or so earlier, we're more "inside" than they are.

Good Raised Up—a way of saying that we've witnessed good actions influenced by a person listening to God's direction—or the advice the speaker has given them. "I saw the good raised up in that young Friend." The phrase comes from a quotation by Robert Barclay: "I found the evil weakening in me, and the good raised up."

Hold in the Light—often what a Quaker says to someone who needs praying for, as in "I'll hold you in the Light," the Light being God's love and care. It is also a way of saying somebody needs to be closer to God, as in "I'm going to be holding him so close to the Light that he's gonna get sunburned." This is not unbiblical: see Paul's injunction in Romans 12:20.

I have a concern—in Quakerese, something is weighing on my soul. Sometimes it's clear. Other times it's more vague—as a sense of unease. "I have a concern for the unrest in the Middle East" is an example of a concern that's clear. "I have a concern for the way this discussion is going" is vaguer and generally means "I don't like the turn we've just taken and am concerned y'all aren't listening to me."

A corollary is when someone says "You obviously carry a strong concern," when what they really mean is "You've been harping on this for months. Give it a rest."

Leadings—clear, distinct direction or guidance coming from God. They are a call to specific action (as compared with a "concern," which may not have a specific action related to it). "I feel a leading to start a new Quaker meeting on the beaches of Waikiki next February" is an example of what a Friend (maybe from Minnesota) might say. The meeting then has to decide if this is a true leading from God or a false leading coming from ego, misdirection, or frigid weather. Several trips to Hawaii might be required before that determination can be made.

Meeting—what we Quakers call church or worship. "I'm going to Meeting" can mean either I'm going to the Meetinghouse (church house) or to worship service. Or it can mean "I'm sleeping in" as it did for my college roommate who named his bunk "Meeting."

That friend speaks my mind—the Friendly way of showing agreement with something another Friend has just said. It is supposed to preclude the need for elaboration on what the first Friend said but often is a prelude for a lengthy addendum indicating why the speaker feels that what the first Friend said is correct.

That's a name (idea, project, etc.) that would not have occurred to me—how we say "Are you out of your mind?!?"

This needs some seasoning—ideally, while the idea or project proposed looks like it might be good, it needs more thought. Of course, saying "The Young Friends' proposal to turn the meetingroom

into a roller derby rink needs some seasoning" is also a way
of saying "If we put it off for six months or so, maybe they'll
forget about the whole thing."

Thy message is received—basically "We heard you. Now sit down and
be quiet."

If you'd like to review other Friendly words and phrases, with
more serious definitions than those above, please visit New York Yearly
Meeting of Friends' "Glossary of Quaker Terms & Concepts" at http://
www.nyym.org/?q=glossary.

ACKNOWLEDGMENTS

"No good deed goes unpunished," as the famous Quaker poet Walt Brownleaf Wittier said, so now I get to out some of the Friendly folks who encouraged (or at least didn't discourage me enough!) in the writing of this book.

First, I want to thank many of the members of the Association of Bad Friends on Facebook. Bunches of you have been enjoying that page and contributing to it for years. On the days when life feels a little gloomy, it's great to visit y'all and come away with a smile—the jokes, the tales you tell on yourselves, the cartoons are great fun. Mostly. Some of you though need severely eldered at times... but you know who you are.

Second, I'd be remiss if I didn't mention Jacob and Gretta Stone. Both are funny (and deep) clear to the bone and, along with my wife, Nancy, were there for the mis-conception of the afore-mentioned Association of Bad Friends. That result shows that there really are some people who should not be left alone together for too long.

Other friends/Friends who have nurtured my funny bone include Nancy Armstrong, Dr. Philip Ball, J. Stanley Banker, John Bill (aka "Dad"), Stephanie Deakin, Howard Macy, the late Tom Mullen, and Aaron Spiegel. Others, too many to name here, have blessed me with their ministry of mirth. Named or unnamed, they've each brought joy into my life—along with laughs and love.

ACKNOWLEDGMENTS

Finally, there's Nancy Elizabeth. For nigh onto thirty years she's laughed (mostly) at my jokes, encouraged my writing, and matched my wit remark by remark. She is wicked funny when she wants to be— which is a good deal of the time. And she's good and kind, too. Thanks, Lizzer.

NOTES

Introduction

"When someone asks me what kind of Christian I am..."

Diana Butler Bass, *A People's History of Christianity: The Other Side of the Story* (New York: Harper Collins Publishers, 2009), 296.

"I call you friends."

John 15:15

"Full armor of God"

Ephesians 6:11 NIV

"Love, joy, peace, forbearance, kindness, goodness, faithfulness..."

Galatians 5:22-23

"Are you still a Quaker?"

https://www.youtube.com/watch?v=oKwlRRv6EiU&feature=youtu.be

1. Just Be Quiet

"There is a quiet, open place in the depths of the mind."

Kenneth E. Boulding, "The Practice of The Love of God" (Philadelphia: Book Committee, Religious Society of Friends, 1942). The 1942 William Penn Lecture delivered at the Arch Street Meetinghouse in Philadelphia, PA. http://pamphlets.quaker.org/wpl1942a.html

NOTES

"Words may help and silence may help."

Caroline Emelia Stephen, *Light Arising: Thoughts on the Central Radiance* (Cambridge: W. Heffner and Son, 1908), 67.

"Listen carefully to what I am about to tell you."

Luke 9:44 NIV

"Shut up, he explained."

Ring W. Lardner Jr., The Young Immigrunts (Indianapolis, IN: Bobbs Merrill Company, 1920), 78.

"In October 1656, Quaker James Nayler..."

William G. Bittle, James Nayler: The Quaker Indicted by Parliament (York, England: William Sessions Ltd, 1986).

"If you don't know the Spurrlows."

http://thurlowspurr.com/alumni-connection.html

"It was eighteen adults settin' in a circle."

https://www.youtube.com/watch?v=rNiibrDYxmM

"For where two or three gather in my name..."

Matthew 18:20

"I am become as sounding brass."

1 Corinthians 13:1 KJV

"Speak. Your servant is listening."

1 Samuel 3:10

"Conducting our inward life."

Thomas Kelly, A Testament of Devotion (New York: Harper & Brothers, 1941), 5.

"True silence is the rest of the mind."

"Advice to His Children" by William Penn, 1699, from A Collection of the Works of William Penn to Which Is Prefixed a Journal of His Life. With Many

Original Letters and Papers Not Before Published, vol. 1 (London: Assigns of J. Sowle, 1726), 899.

"[I] walked again up the street."

Benjamin Franklin, *The Autobiography of Benjamin Franklin*, The Electric Ben Franklin, http://www.ushistory.org/franklin/autobiography/page12.htm

"Come to me."

Matthew 11:28

"Is living, active and sharper."

Hebrews 4:12

"The contemplative."

Thomas Merton, *New Seeds of Contemplation* (New York: New Directions Books, 1961), 9.

"Contemplation is...the response to a call."

Ibid.

2. World at War

"We utterly deny all outward wars and strife and fightings."

George Fox et al., *A Declaration from the Harmless and Innocent People of God Called Quakers, Against All Plotters and Fighters in the World*. Presented to King Charles on November 21, 1660. Commonly referred to as "A Declaration to Charles II," http://www.qhpress.org/quakerpages/qwhp/dec1660.htm

"Our life is love, and peace, and tenderness."

Miscellaneous Letters of Isaac Penington, ed. John Barclay (Philadelphia: Friends Book Store, 1828), 139.

"Happy are people who make peace."

Matthew 5:9

"You can't say that civilization don't advance."

Will Rogers, *New York Times*, December 23, 1929.

"I mean, during my…"

National Archives, Statistical Information about Fatal Casualties of the Vietnam War, http://www.archives.gov/research/military/vietnam-war /casualty-statistics.html

"Two of those killed weren't…" May 4 Task Force, "The Slain: William Knox Schroeder," http://dept.kent.edu/may4/bill.html. Also "The Report of the President's Commission on-Campus Unrest," http://files.eric.ed.gov /fulltext/ED083899.pdf

"Whoever can reconcile this, 'Resist not evil.'"

Robert Barclay, *Apology for the True Christian Divinity* (London: 1678), 401–2.

"There is a popular faith."

Josiah Strong, *Our Country: Its Possible Future and Its Present Crisis* (New York: Baker & Taylor for the American Home Missionary Society, 1885), 30.

"Nathanael Greene (1742–1786)…"

New George Encyclopedia, "Nathanael Greene (1742-1786)," http://www .georgiaencyclopedia.org/articles/history-archaeology/nathanael-greene -1742-1786

"I believe there is more thought and attention."

Daniel Hill, Fifth Annual Report of the Secretary of the Peace Association of Friends in America as recorded in *Minutes of Western Yearly Meeting of Friends*, 1870 (Indianapolis: J. G. Doughty, 1870), 62.

"I expect to *pass through* this world but once."

Stephen Grellet as quoted in W. Gurney Benham, *A Book of Quotations, Proverbs and Household Words* (Philadelphia: J. B. Lippincott, 1914), 448.

"The haunting fear that *someone, somewhere…*"

H. L. Mencken, *A Mencken Chrestomathy: His Own Selection of His Choicest Writings* (New York: A. A. Knopf, 1949), 624.

"God is not alone the God…"

Christian Faith and Practice in the Experience of the Society of Friends (London: London Yearly Meeting of the Religious Society of Friends, 1959, no. 605 quoting the "All Friends Conference of 1920."

"Delights to do no evil."

"His Last Testimony" from A Collection of Sundry Books, Epistles and Papers Written by James Nayler (London: Assigns of J. Sowle, 1716), xxxvii.

"In 1828, theological and other tensions…"

H. Larry Ingle, Quakers in Conflict: The Hicksite Reformation (Knoxville: University of Tennessee Press, 1986), 237–42.

"Let us then try what Love will do."

William Penn, Some Fruits of Solitude (Scottsdale, PA: Herald Press, 2003), 115.

"All shall be well…"

Julian of Norwich, http://justus.anglican.org/resources/bio/154.html

"Peace begins within ourselves."

Sydney Bailey, Peace Is a Process (London: Quaker Books, 1993), 173.

3. To Buy or Not to Buy

"Simplicity is the name."

Lloyd Lee Wilson, "Discernment: Coming Under the Guidance of the Holy Spirit," North Carolina Yearly Meeting (Conservative) Journal, no. 6 (n.p., 2012), 2.

"Living simply is the right ordering."

http://www.afsc.org/testimonies/simplicity

"Therefore I say to you."

Matthew 6:25

"Progress is man's ability."

Thor Heyerdahl quoted in Richard R. Lineman, "Two-Way Ticket to Paradise," review of *Fatu-Hiva* by Thor Heyerdah, *New York Times*, August 29, 1975.

" 'Tis the gift to be simple, 'tis the gift to be free"
Words and music by Elder Joseph Brackett.

"When my parents came for their first visit..."
Mark Burch, remarks as part of the Quaker Study: "Come All Ye Who are Heavily Cumbered: Simplicity as the Radical Path to Peace, Justice, Community and Care of the Earth" presented at Canadian Yearly Meeting, 2014.

"On June 21, 1933, John Dillinger..."
Dary Matera, *John Dillinger: America's First Celebrity Criminal* (New York: Avalon, 2004).

"But Christ Jesus said."
http://www.hallvworthington.com/Margaret_Fox_Selections/MargaretMiscLetters.html

"Woolman, unlike me, was a good Quaker..."
Thomas P. Slaughter, *The Beautiful Soul of John Woolman: Apostle of Abolition* (New York: Hill and Wang, 2008).

"And they shall beat their swords."
Isaiah 2:4 KJV

"Turn all the treasures we possess."
John Woolman, "A Plea for the Poor, Or A Word of Remembrance and Caution to the Rich" in *The Journal and Major Essays of John Woolman*, ed. Phillips P. Moulton (New York: Oxford University Press, 1971), 241.

"Our gracious Creator cares."
Ibid.

"May we look upon our treasures."
Ibid., 255.

"It is estimated that the DRC..."

University of Michigan, "Coltan Mining in the Democratic Republic of Congo," http://sitemaker.umich.edu/section002group3/coltan_mining_in _democratic_republic_of_the_congo

"It is easy to let ourselves slip."

http://kingston.quaker.ca/Quotes.htm

4. Red and Yellow, Black and White

"Guided by the Light of God within."

Meg Maslin quoted in *Quaker Faith and Practice*, 2nd ed. (London: The Yearly Meeting of the Religious Society of Friends in Britain, 1999), no. 23:33.

"My activism did not spring from my being gay."

I Must Resist: Bayard Rustin's Life in Letters, ed. Michael G. Long (San Francisco: City Lights Books, 2012), 460.

"Answering that of God in everyone."

Journal of George Fox, ed. John L. Nickalls (London: London Yearly Meeting of the Religious Society of Friends, 1975), 263.

"A man went down from Jerusalem to Jericho."

Luke 10:30–36

"There is nothing more dangerous."

"Election Speech, 1904" in G.B.S. 90: *Aspects of George Bernard Shaw's Life and Work*, ed. Stephen Winsten (New York: Dodd, Mead and Company, 1946), 155.

"Red and yellow, black and white"

"Jesus Loves the Little Children," words by C. Herbert Woolston, music by George F. Root.

"walk cheerfully over the earth..."

The Journal of George Fox, http://www.hallvworthington.com/wjournal /gfjournal4c.html "all 7+ billion of us..."

U.S. and World Population Clock, http://www.census.gov/popclock/

"Don't think of yourself."

Romans 12:3

"Samuel Johnson expressed his..."

The Samuel Johnson Sound Bite Page, no. 53, http://www.samueljohnson.com/expectat.html

"There is neither Jew nor Greek."

Galatians 3:28

"In 1658 Mary Fisher felt led..."

Marcelle Martin, "Mary Fisher: Maidservant Turned Prophet," *Friends Journal,* http://www.friendsjournal.org/2008017/

"I don't know what I'm doing."

Romans 7:15, 18-19

"some Friends' meetings had benches..."

Donna McDaniel and Vanessa Julye, *Fit for Freedom, Not for Friendship: Quakers, African Americans and the Myth of Racial Justice* (Philadelphia: Quaker Books of FGC, 2009), 194–98.

"Studies show that people..."

"A Serving of Gratitude May Save the Day," *New York Times,* Nov. 21, 2011, http://www.nytimes.com/2011/11/22/science/a-serving-of-gratitude -brings-healthy-dividends.html?_r=0

"Any immigrant who lives with you."

Leviticus 19:34

"On the Muncie, Indiana, Friends Memorial Church..."

Dwight W. Hoover, "Daisy Douglas Barr: From Quaker to Klan 'Kluckeress'" *Indiana Magazine of History* (June 1991). http://scholarworks .iu.edu/journals/index.php/imh/article/viewFile/11137/15984

"If you were blind."
John 9:41

5. Truth Be Told

"Integrity is a condition."
Kenneth C. Barnes, *The Future of the Society of Friends* (London: Friends Home Service Committee, 1972), 26–27.

"The family is a place to practise."
Elizabeth Watson, "Parents and Children in the Quaker Home," *Canadian Friend* 75, no. 5 (September-October 1979): 14–15.

"Let your *yes* be yes."
Matthew 5:37

"Though I am not naturally honest."
Autolycus in William Shakespeare, *A Winter's Tale.*

"The early Quakers called themselves…"
John 15:15

"Again, you have heard…"
Matthew 5:33-37

"They also built a model village…"
Bournville Village Trust, https://www.bvt.org.uk/our-business/the
-history-and-ethos-of-bournville/

"Whittaker Chambers was both a Quaker…"
H. Larry Ingle, "Richard Nixon, Whittaker Chambers, Alger Hiss, and Quakerism," *Quaker History* 101, no. 1 (Spring 2012): 1–11.

"*Open my ears.*"
Clara H. Scott, *"Open My Eyes,"* 1895.

"I told him that I had read it."
Reminiscences of Levi Coffin (Cincinnati: Robert Clarke & Co., 1880). http://docsouth.unc.edu/nc/coffin/coffin.html

"A company of seventeen fugitives."

Ibid.

"Buy one from a Quaker."

Philip Gulley, *For Everything a Season: Simple Musings on Living Well* (New York: HarperCollins, 2001), 147.

"If we would indeed take a place"

Quoted by Marshall Massey, as from a document by the London Yearly Meeting [Discipline] Revision Committee in 1925. https://www.facebook .com/marshall.massey/posts/10150934617045896?fref=nf

"Truthiness is 'What I say is right.'"

Nathan Rabin, "Stephen Colbert," Jan. 25, 2006, http://www.avclub.com/ article/stephen-colbert-13970

"Before the world was."

George Fox, "Epistle no. 149" (1657). http://www.qhpress.org/texts /oldqwhp/gf-e-toc.htm

"Jesus saw the truth."

George B. Jeffery, *Christ Yesterday and Today* (London: George Allen and Unwin, 1934), 47.

6. God's Good Green Earth

"The produce of the earth."

"Conversations on the True Harmony of Mankind" in *The Journal and Essays of John Woolman*, ed. A. M. Gummere (New York: n.p., 1922), 4625.

"As a Religious Society of Friends."

Minute 25 of London Yearly Meeting as recorded in *London Yearly Meeting Proceedings*, 1988, 262.

"You will love your neighbor."

Mark 12:31

"There will be a rain dance."

George Carlin, *The Merv Griffin Show*, Aug. 31, 1965. https://www
.youtube.com/watch?v=fyzBO_etwko

"That's because about 130 people a year…"

http://www.public-health.uiowa.edu/gpcah/resources/pdf/GPCAH
_tractor_overturns_2014.pdf

"I still find each day too short."

John Burroughs, *The Writings of John Burroughs*, vol. 15: *The Summit of the
Years* (New York: Houghton Mifflin Company, 1913), v.

"That's why so many Friends…"

Charlotte Alter, *Time*, "Hundreds of Thousands Converge on New
York to Demand Climate-Change Action" (Sept. 21, 2014). http://time
.com/3415162/peoples-climate-march-new-york-manhattan-demonstration/

"Ever since I was a little girl."

Katherine Murray, e-mail to author, September 1, 2014.

"I'd been growing increasingly concerned."

Eileen Flanagan, e-mail to author, August 18, 2014.

"Quakers dominated…"

"Quakers and Whaling," http://www.quakersintheworld.org/quakers-in
-action/198

"Own naturally based cleaning products"

Such as this one: http://www.accidentallygreen.com/making-your-own
-safe-bathroom-cleaners

"The effectual fervent prayer."

James 5:16 KJV

"The earth is the LORD's."

Psalm 24:1

"And God blessed them."

Genesis 1:28 KJV

"You must keep my decrees and my laws."

Leviticus 18:26, 28 NIV

"One report says that 30 percent…"

Africa Files, "DR Congo: The coltan phenomenon," http://www.africafiles.org/article.asp?ID=924

"The United States, for example."

World Population Balance, http://www.worldpopulationbalance.org/population_energy

"Think what forty thousand dollars…"

Tom Vanden Brook, "Cost of bombing ISIL cheap compared with Afghan War," *USA Today*, Sept. 26, 2014, http://www.usatoday.com/story/news/world/2014/09/25/war-costs-syria-afghanistan/16211545/

"Of which there are…"

No Kid Hungry, http://www.nokidhungry.org/problem/hunger-facts

"All species and the Earth itself."

Audrey Urry quoted in *Quaker Faith and Practice*, 2nd ed. (London: The Yearly Meeting of the Religious Society of Friends in Britain, 1999), no. 25:04.

7. Walking Cheerfully

"Be patterns, be examples."

Journal of George Fox, ed. John L. Nickalls (London: London Yearly Meeting of the Religious Society of Friends, 1975), 263.

"In his cool sunglasses."

Gretta Stone, "The Foxy George Song" copyright 2002. http://www.pym.org/pastoral-care-newsletter/files/2012/12/Volume-14-Issue-04.pdf.

"You filter out an ant."

Matthew 23:24

"Seriousness is the only refuge."

Oscar Wilde quoted in *1,911 Best Things Anybody Ever Said*, comp. Robert Byrne (New York: Fawcett Columbine, 1988), no. 71.

"William Rathbone..."

Irving and Ruth Verlenden Poley, *Friendly Anecdotes* (New York: Harper & Brothers, 1946), 26.

"Walk cheerfully over the world."

Journal of George Fox, ed. John L. Nickalls (London: London Yearly Meeting of the Religious Society of Friends, 1975), 263.

"God loves a cheerful giver."

2 Corinthians 9:7

"'Shout louder!' he said."

1 Kings 18:27 NIV

"The Bible is often funny."

Howard Macy, *Laughing Pilgrims: Humor and the Spiritual Journey* (Waynesboro, GA: Paternoster Press, 2006), 89.

"To do with all of life."

Ibid., 3.

"Humor can be dissected."

E. B. White, "Some Remarks on Humor" in *A Subtreasury of American Humor*, ed. E. B. White and Katherine S. White (New York: Modern Library, 1941), xvii.

"John Salkeld, an eighteenth-century Quaker..."

Irving and Ruth Verlenden Poley, *Friendly Anecdotes* (New York: Harper & Brothers, 1946), 24.

"No morons so play the fool."

Desiderious Erasmus, *The Praise of Folly*, trans. Hoyt Hopewell Hudson (New York: Modern Library, 1941).

"Go eat rich food."

Nehemiah 8:10

8: Closing Deep Thoughts...

"You are my friends..."

John 15:14

Appendix 2: The Good, the Bad, and the Quakers

There are a variety of sources for this information. You can find them (and more Quaker personalities—such as me!) at:

Adherents.com's "Famous Friends (Famous Quakers)," http://www.adherents.com/largecom/fam_quaker.html

Conservative Friend's "Quakers: Famous and Infamous," http://www.conservativefriend.org/quakersfamousandinfamous.htm

Mental Floss's "Richard Nixon and 12 Other Celebrity Quakers," http://mentalfloss.com/article/17732/richard-nixon-and-12-other-celebrity-quakers (I didn't make this list. Sigh!)

Wikipedia's "List of Quakers," http://en.wikipedia.org/wiki/List_of_Quakers

Appendix 4: Some Good Advices

"Too many times we pray for ease..."

Philip J. Gulley, *Front Porch Tales* (San Francisco: Harper San Francisco, 2007), 19.

"There is a spirit which I feel that delights to do no evil..."

James Nayler, *A Collection of Sundry Books, Epistles, and Papers* (n.p. 1716), 696.

"Words may help and silence may help…"
Caroline Stephen, *Light Arising: Thoughts on the Central Radiance* (Cambridge: W. Heffner and Sons, 1908), 67.

"Inner silence, calming the agitations of our hearts and minds…"
http://universalistfriends.org/seeger-04.html

"The likeness we bear to Jesus is more essential…"
Anna Davis Hallowell, editor, *James and Lucretia Mott: Life and Letters* (Boston: Houghton, Miflin and Co., 1896), 526.

"The discovery of God lies in the daily and the ordinary…"
Richard J. Foster, *Prayer: Finding The Heart's True Home* (San Francisco: Harper San Francisco, 1992), 171.

"Friends come back from their worship…"
http://quakerquotes.com/2014/11/15/a-quote-on-quaker-worship-rufus-jones-1863-1948/

"Contemporary Christians find…"
Sandra L. Cronk, *Dark Night Journey: Inward Re-patterning Toward a Life Centered in God* (Wallingford, PA: Pendle Hill Publications, 1991).

"To me, being a Christian is a particular way of life…"
James Hough, editor, *The Christian Life Lived Experimentally: An Anthology of the Writings of Kathleen Lonsdale* (London: Friends Home Service Committee, 1976), 17-18.

"What is the Quaker faith?"
Elise Boulding, *The Quaker Journey: A Talk with Students* (Philadelphia: Friends General Conference, 1961).

"The one cornerstone of belief upon which the Society of Friends is built…"
Caroline E. Stephen, *Quaker Strongholds* (London: Kegan Paul, Trench, Trübner and Company, Ltd, 1890), 20.

"From this fog-bound Earth of ours…"

http://growinggracefarm.com/tag/peace/

"Our life is love, and peace, and tenderness…"
http://www.qhpress.org/texts/penington/letter20.html

"If fighting is inconsistent with an ideal society…"
http://www.qcea.org/wp-content/uploads/2011/04/ar-qcea-en-2007.
pdf

"Only the inner vision of God…"
"Holy Obedience," William Penn Lecture, 1939. http://pamphlets.quaker.
org/wpl1939.pdf

"Quakers are not 'for peace'…"
Ben Pink Dandelion, *Celebrating the Quaker Way* (London: Britain Yearly
Meeting, 2009).

"The moral man is he who is opposed to injustice…"
"In Apprehension How Like a God!" William Penn Lecture, 1948. http://
pamphlets.quaker.org/wpl1948a.html

"Quaker…'concerns' are usually personal…"
http://rjtechne.org/quakers/quaker350/quotes.htm

"Eternal God, let thy spirit inspire and guide us…"
"Prayer of Pierre Ceresole," translation in *The Friend*, volume 104 (London:
1946), 2.

"The only way to seek God is to seek God first."
"The Flavor of Man," William Penn Lecture, 1949. http://pamphlets.
quaker.org/wpl1949a.html

"We know that the principles of our faith teach…"
"The Light Within as Redemptive Power," William Penn Lecture, 1945.
http://pamphlets.quaker.org/wpl1945a.html

"Dear Lord and Father of mankind…"

John Greenleaf Whittier, *The Complete Poetical Works of John Greenleaf Whittier* (Boston: James R. Osgood and Company, 1876), 373.

"There is a daily round for beauty..."

Caroline C. Graveson, *Religion and Culture* (London: George Allen & Unwin, 1937), 24-25.

"We are lured toward truth, beauty, and goodness..."

Haven Kimmel, *The Solace Of Leaving Early* (New York: Anchor Books, 2002), 34.

"Oh Lord, may I be directed what to do and what to leave undone."

Katherine Fry and Rachel Elizabeth Fry Creswell, editors, *Memoir of the Life of Elizabeth Fry* (Philadelphia: J. W. Moore, 1847), 307.

"To live our faith and not merely proclaim it..."

Scott Russell Sanders, *The Force of Spirit* (Boston: Beacon Press, 2000), 35.

"First, we all have an inner teacher whose guidance is more reliable..."

Parker J. Palmer, *A Hidden Wholeness: The Journey Toward an Undivided Life* (San Francisco: Jossey-Bass, 2004), 25-26.

"The unity of Christians..."

Thomas Story, *Discourse in the Meeting at Horselydown, on the 26th Day of February, 1737; Concerning the Diversity of Opinions and Divisions in Religion, Still Subsisting in the Christian World* (n.c.: n.p., 1737), title page.

"A true Friends' meeting for worship..."

No time but this present (Birmingham, England: Friends World Committee for Consultation, 1967), 110-11.

"A religious awakening which does not awaken..."

http://www.qotd.org/search/search.html?aid=3506

"It is for this grace that we pray..."

Phyllis Richards, "What do ye to excess?" in *The Friend*, volume 107 (1948): 306.

Appendix 5: How to Talk Quaker

"Dialect—noun…"

http://www.merriam-webster.com/dictionary/dialect

"I found the evil weakening…"

Robert Barclay, *Apology for the True Christian Divinity*, Proposition 11, Section 7.

About Brent

In addition to his ministry of writing, Brent also enjoys a ministry of leading workshops and speaking. These are some of his most popular topics.

The Sacred Compass: Spiritual Practices for Discernment is a workshop for those who want to learn discernment as a life process.
Writing from the Heart: Telling Your Soul's Stories is for those who want to unlock their spiritual stories.
Awaken Your Senses (with Beth Booram) is geared toward helping people experience God in new ways by using their bodies and souls.
Being Quiet: The Practice of Holy Silence is based on Quaker silence and teaches how to be quiet and still in our souls amidst the clamor of everyday life.

If you would like more information about Brent's writing, his spirituality workshops and retreats, or would like to contact him about other speaking engagements, you can reach him through his website at www.brentbill.com or via e-mail at brentbil@brentbill.com.
You can read new material and see photography by Brent at holyordinary.blogspot.com.

"Friend,
I would not harm thee
for the world,
but thee is standing
where I am about to
shoot," says the Friendly
farmer in the old Quaker
joke. Today's joke
is, harm or no,
the world is standing
where we are
shooting,
Friend.

CPSIA information can be obtained
at www.ICGtesting.com
Printed in the USA
LVHW031908090719
623603LV00003B/3/P